WOJTEK'S BISTRO

Recipes from a Polish Kitchen

WOJTEK VAN PORTEK

MITCHELL BEAZLEY

HOLIDAY
NEW
YORK

CONTENTS

WELCOME TO WOJTEK'S BISTRO

I have a memory of being in rural Poland, years ago, in my grandmother's vegetable garden on a hot August day. The air was tomato-scented, and all around there was bounty: purple plums hung heavy on the trees, pumpkins were turning orange and cucumbers were waiting to be pickled. I didn't know it at the time, but that garden, her home and her kitchen was to shape my culinary education. Recipes were rarely written down and there were certainly no photographs, so watching her cook, and later listening to her relaying her recipes to me over the phone as I struggled to recreate her 'feeling' in my London kitchen, was the best cookery school I could ask for. What I learned went beyond how to cook. Her examples showed me generosity and resourcefulness; she gave me courage to be daring and inventive, but most of all she showed me that good food isn't about fancy ingredients. This was her culinary heritage, and I took it upon myself to keep it alive.

When I moved to London for my MA, I came armed with jars of her homemade passata and preserves. Eating well and cheaply wasn't as straightforward as it had been back home. The multicultural food scene was mind-boggling, yet what I really craved were the straightforward, familiar flavours of my grandmother's kitchen that I'd taken for granted my whole life. And so, a cook was born.

Solo dinners evolved into my version of fine dining on a fashion worker's salary. Phone calls home helped me create simple but sublime meals, which I served on flea-market plates mixed with my grandmother's inherited crockery.

When my grandmother died, the void was immeasurable. Worse than the sadness was the silence. There were no more calls to check a recipe, no more discussions about secret ingredients. I clung to the jars of rose petal jam she'd made, as if they somehow embodied her. But then I remembered all that she had taught me, the legacy that has shaped how I cook now.

From her, I learned that cooking is about sharing. I learned to work with what I had and to respect the rhythm of the seasons. Measurements were not always required; what mattered was flavour and abundance on every plate. I realized that the knowledge had transferred, and I could cook, even in London, even without her.

What began as 'Wojtek's Bistro for one' grew when friends started begging me for invites. Then Instagram took notice. Before long, people were asking me to cater for their business lunches and marriage proposals.

This book bridges two worlds: honouring my grandmother's Polish flavours while embracing London's vibrant food culture. It's about my journey from a bountiful kitchen garden in Poland to a small East London kitchen, where pierogi meet British ingredients, and where my grandmother's spirit lives on in every recipe. Whether traditional or updated with new flavours, I know she would approve.

Interview

KEY INGREDIENTS

When you grow up around your grandmother's cooking, what makes it all so wonderful is not always evident. Living in another country, however, has made it blindingly obvious to me, and I now know that certain ingredients aren't just pantry staples – they form the soul of Polish flavours.

Allspice – If a dish was cooked in Poland and savoury, there's a high probability it contains one of these little brown berries. The spiciness is similar to black pepper but with more warmth.

Bay leaves – Possibly the national herb of Poland, usually used fresh. One is rarely enough and many recipes call for several.

Butter – Alongside sunflower oil, butter is the main cooking fat in Poland. Always unsalted, often clarified, like ghee.

Dill – This herb grew like a weed in my grandmother's garden. If there were boiled potatoes, there was dill on top, no exceptions.

Dried mushrooms – Wild mushroom flavour is essential in Poland. With an abundance of forests, mushroom foraging is a favourite pastime.

Pickled cucumbers – Crunchy, tangy *ogórki* appear at most Polish meals. There are three main kinds: sour brine fermented (*kiszone*); half-sour lightly fermented (*malosolne*), and vinegar

Bay leaves

Butter

Dried prunes

pickles (*konserwowe*), which are mainly used in this book. French cornichons would generally be a good substitute for vinegar pickles if necessary.

Pistachios – I cannot help but think of my grandmother when I see pistachios, because she passed her love of them on to me. This ingredient is not particular to Poland, but they are significant in my cooking.

Polish bacon – Sold as thick, very fatty slabs that are almost always smoked. The rendered fat is used for everything from frying onions to making pierogi.

Prunes – These wrinkly gems pop up everywhere, and in Poland you can also find smoked prunes. I always have at least one bag of these in my pantry.

Sauerkraut – I can still picture massive jars fermenting in my grandmother's cellar, the smell somehow both off-putting and delightful at the same time. If you want to cook Polish cuisine, you must have jars of this tangy cabbage for soups, stews and salads.

Sweet paprika – This is not the spicy kind – Polish cooks prefer a gentle, sweet flavour, and this spice provides great colour in cooking, too.

Vanilla pods in vodka – My grandmother always had vanilla bean pods steeping in vodka and I have maintained this tradition. The pods become plumper, and the vanilla-infused vodka is a lovely bonus.

Dried prunes, pistachios, paprika and allspice berries

Sauerkraut

Vanilla pods in vodka

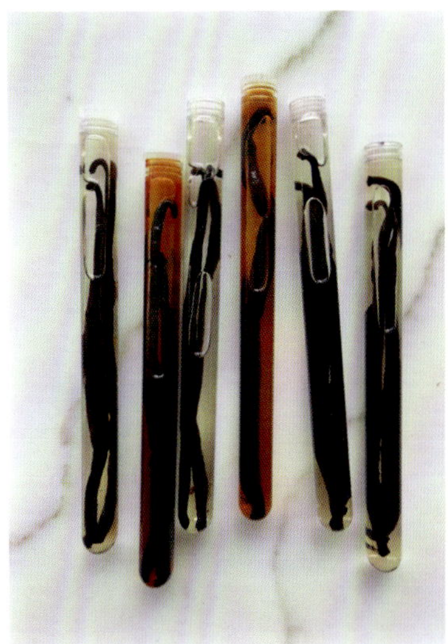

SERVING IN STYLE

My philosophy is this: every day deserves to be a celebration, and the way a table looks is every bit as important as the food you serve. I have noticed that something remarkable happens when you sit down at a beautifully dressed table, and it is this: a meal transforms from simple necessity into full-blown enjoyment. This transformation is at the heart of what I try to achieve at my supper club, Wojtek's Bistro, and I hope you will try creating this in your own home, not just for special occasions, but every single day. Here are my key principles:

Abundance over perfection – have confidence to mix things rather than worry about absolute symmetry. I've never believed that everything must coordinate exactly. Real beauty has an element of imperfection, and the unexpected. Once you accept this, you'll never look at your dining table the same way again.

Every day deserves celebration – A Tuesday night supper deserves just as much attention as a birthday celebration. Both are worthy of thoughtfully chosen table linen, your nicest plates and fresh flowers. This isn't about being formal or fussy. Why save your beautiful things for company? Enjoy them daily – that's what they're for.

Transform the ordinary – A simple bowl of soup, when lovingly prepared, doesn't deserve to be gulped down in front of the TV. Take the time to set a place for yourself at a table, fold a proper napkin and choose a beautiful bowl to serve it in. These small acts of attention will elevate the entire experience. You're not just eating, you're dining, and there's a huge difference.

Ambience matters – Once I began setting the table regularly, even when alone, I realized I was on to something. Just a napkin and a proper glass made me feel like I was in an elegant restaurant. You don't need a reason to create an ambience, you just need intention, a good eye and a collection of pretty plates and glasses.

Clockwise from top left, 1: Once you start collecting mismatched crystal, there is no going back. **2:** A return from the flower market sets up expectations of the bouquets for the week ahead. **3:** When flowers fade, shortened stems become an attractive centrepiece. **4:** Teapots and flowers at Wojtek's Bistro.

Clockwise from top left, 1: Antique glassware is always in use on my table. **2:** Hand-painted serving plates and vintage glasses and cutlery are both beautiful and functional. **3:** Single blossoms past their best are still radiant in old crystal. **4:** In my element at a French flea market, demonstrating the art of mismatching.

TABLE-SETTING TIPS

My work has taken me around the world, and I've collected pieces everywhere I've travelled. Not necessarily from expensive boutiques, but from antique markets and wonderful little shops tucked away in unexpected places. When I see a beautiful plate or an interesting glass, I am captivated by the object itself. I have no desire to find matching items or complete a set number.

Avoid coordinating items – I'm completely opposed to what I call rigid, matchy-matchy table settings. When everything is too coordinated, too perfect, it feels contrived and frankly, uninviting. True style comes from thoughtful combinations of colours, textures and forms. When you are arranging a table setting, consider all the senses: think about its visual appeal, but also texture, fragrance and how things feel in your hand. Elements that might seem to clash individually can create something genuinely beautiful when brought together. This unique sense of style results in beautiful, interesting pieces that look wonderful together precisely because you chose them, not because they were designed to match.

Choose flowers to suit your mood – As well as fresh ingredients on a plate, fresh flowers on the table are a must for me. They connect the natural world to your carefully crafted indoor environment, which is especially important during a meal. I love all flowers, but when choosing, I like to consider the mood I want to convey. For big and bold I like to choose sunflowers, hydrangeas, dahlias and peonies. For something more subtle and subdued, I would choose zinnias, spray roses, sweet peas or a tulip or two. Always trim stems before arranging, change the water regularly and keep flowers out of direct sunlight.

The vase matters – When it comes to arranging flowers for a table, think about the container as carefully as the flowers themselves. Whether it's a vintage vessel or a simple copper pot, it's important to get the height and volume right for your arrangement. A wide, shallow vase is perfect for several loud and blousy blooms, other times you may prefer a single stem in a small, short vessel, just below eye level. And to keep the party going, when blooms are past their prime, trim the best stems and arrange them in wine glasses or float flower heads in small bowls scattered around the table – these miniature arrangements can still bring tremendous joy.

CHAPTER 1

SMALL PLATES

MINI STEAK TARTARE

This is undeniably French, but it's a staple of Polish tables, too. I wasn't a big fan of homemade tartare until two people changed my mind: my paternal grandmother's cook, and my friend Jan, who finally convinced me to try making it myself. The golden rule? Always mince the beef yourself because it's about freshness and quality. Use the best beef from a reliable source, keep everything cold and mince it just before serving. Once you taste this done properly, there's no going back.

SERVES 4

350g (12oz) top-quality beef fillet or sirloin, preferably frozen for 30 minutes (see Note)
1 tablespoon finely chopped shallot
1 tablespoon capers, finely chopped
1 Polish gherkin, finely chopped, plus extra to serve
1-3 anchovy fillets, finely chopped
1-2 sun-dried tomatoes in oil, drained and finely chopped
½ teaspoon Dijon mustard
1 egg yolk
¼ teaspoon salt
Worcestershire sauce, to taste
freshly ground black pepper

TO GARNISH
whole caperberries
pickled red onion (see page 214 for homemade)
Tabasco sauce

Cut the beef into 4 pieces; smaller pieces make hand-mincing easier. Start with one piece and, using a sharp knife, cut into matchsticks, then slice across the matchsticks to obtain a fine mince. Repeat with the remaining beef pieces.

Put the minced beef with all the remaining ingredients into a mixing bowl and mix together well. Taste and adjust the seasoning, adding more salt or Worcestershire sauce as desired. Shape into 4 patties and refrigerate until well chilled and ready to serve.

Serve with the garnishes in pretty bowls and a bottle of Tabasco on the table.

NOTE: Buy the best whole cut of meat you can, preferably from a butcher. Putting it in the freezer about 30 minutes before you are ready to mince keeps it cold and helps with the chopping.

CANNELLINI BEAN TOASTS

A vaguely Polish version of hummus, this is also a reflection of my grandmother's love of beans in every way. Serve this spread on toasts or mound in a bowl surrounded by crackers and offer with an aperitif along with olives and nuts. The pickles add the perfect Polish touch.

SERVES 2–4

1 head of garlic, halved horizontally
400g (14oz) can cannellini beans, drained
½ teaspoon extra virgin olive oil, plus extra (optional) to serve
½ teaspoon cider vinegar or freshly squeezed lemon juice
pinch of smoked salt
2–3 Polish pickled cucumbers in vinegar (*konserwowe*), finely chopped (see page 205 for homemade)
a few dill sprigs, finely chopped
freshly ground black pepper
toasted bread slices, to serve

Preheat the oven to 200°C, 180°C fan (400°F), Gas Mark 6.

Wrap the garlic in foil and roast on the oven shelf for about 30 minutes until tender. Remove from the oven and leave to cool.

When cool enough to handle, squeeze the roasted garlic cloves from their skins into a mixing bowl, add the beans and mash well with a fork until blended. Alternatively, for a smooth purée, use a food processor or blender. Add the oil and vinegar or lemon juice and mix or blitz to combine. Season with the smoked salt and pepper to taste.

Mix the pickled cucumbers and dill together in a small bowl.

Spread the bean mixture on toasted bread slices and top with spoonfuls of the chopped pickle and dill. Drizzle with more olive oil, if desired, and serve.

SMOKED MACKEREL SPREAD

This is a wonderfully nostalgic old-school Polish classic slightly updated. Back in the day, this would have been drowning in mayo with chopped egg mixed throughout, but here I've kept it pure and rich, then crowned it with a jammy oeuf mayo for a gorgeous garnish. The result? Perfect balance, beautiful presentation and a dish that my grandmother would have loved.

SERVES 4

300g (10½oz) smoked mackerel fillets
80g (3oz) Polish pickled cucumbers in vinegar (*konserwowe*), finely chopped, (see page 205 for homemade)
50g (1¾oz) shallot, finely chopped
½ apple, cored and grated
1 teaspoon fine salt
1 teaspoon coarsely ground black pepper, plus extra to serve
2 tablespoons good-quality mayonnaise (see page 204 for homemade), plus extra to serve
lemon juice, to taste (optional)
curly parsley sprigs, to garnish

TO SERVE
4 toasted bread slices
2 hard-boiled eggs, shelled and halved

Shred the mackerel into small pieces, discarding the skin. Put into a mixing bowl, add all the remaining ingredients except the lemon juice and mix together well, then leave to stand for 15 minutes. Taste and adjust the seasoning, adding lemon juice to taste if desired.

Spread on the toasted bread slices. Place a hard-boiled egg half in the centre of each toast and top with an extra blob of mayonnaise, then add a good grinding of pepper. Garnish with curly parsley sprigs and serve.

BURRATA WITH VERMOUTH CHERRIES

Cherries macerated in alcohol are a staple in Poland, and I have a memory of my grandmother sitting around with her girlfriends enjoying each other's company and eating ice cream doused in her boozy cherries. In London, I replace the ice cream with a mound of burrata, and I like to use vermouth, as its colour and flavour go remarkably well with cherries. Although simple, you need top-quality ingredients to make this shine: ripe cherries, the best burrata and good vermouth. Any leftover cherry-macerating liquor makes a wonderful spritz with soda water, or use it for cocktails.

SERVES 2–4 AS A STARTER

250g (9oz) cherries, halved and pitted
100ml (3½fl oz) good-quality red vermouth
2 tablespoons sugar
1–2 tablespoons rice vinegar, to taste
2 x 125g (4½oz) balls of burrata cheeses
2 tablespoons extra virgin olive oil
40g (1½oz) shelled pistachio nuts, crushed
salt and freshly ground black pepper
2 basil leaves, to garnish

Put the cherries, vermouth and sugar into a small saucepan and bring just to a simmer over a low heat, stirring gently to dissolve the sugar. Do not boil.

Remove from the heat, stir in the vinegar and leave to cool. (You can prepare the cherries up to 5 days in advance, cover and refrigerate until needed, then bring to room temperature to serve.)

To serve, place each burrata in the centre of a shallow dish and score a shallow cross in the centre of each with a sharp knife. Spoon the cherries around. Drizzle 1 tablespoon of oil over each burrata, then sprinkle half the pistachios over each. Season lightly with salt and pepper and garnish each one with a basil leaf.

BAKED PEAR WITH ROQUEFORT & BACON

A delightful and dramatic starter, the baked Roquefort oozes deliciously out of the pear when it is sliced into, so be sure to have crusty bread on hand to mop up all the juices. This salty-sweet dish is also delectable served with a lightly dressed salad of bitter winter leaves, such as frisée (curly endive), escarole, radicchio or chicory (Belgian endive). My grandmother made hers with Gorgonzola, so you could try that, too.

SERVES 4

4 just-ripe Williams or Comice pears
70g (2½oz) Roquefort cheese
12 or 16 unsmoked bacon rashers (see Note)
2 teaspoons clear honey
freshly ground black pepper
curly parsley sprigs, to garnish

Preheat the oven to 200°C, 180°C fan (400°F), Gas Mark 6. Line a baking tray with nonstick baking paper.

Core the pears from the base with an apple corer, taking care not to go all the way to the stalk; the fruit needs to stay intact. Peel the pears.

Divide the cheese into 4 pieces and stuff the cavity of each pear with a piece of cheese.

Working with one pear at a time on a clean work surface, arrange 3 or 4 bacon rashers crossing each other in a star pattern. Place the pear, sitting upright, in the centre of the star, then drizzle with ½ teaspoon of the honey. Bring the bacon rashers up to the stalk end to enclose the pear and secure at the top with a cocktail stick, or use the stalk. You may need to gently stretch or adjust the bacon rashers to close any gaps and ensure the pear is fully covered.

Stand the pears on the lined tray and season with pepper. Bake for 15–20 minutes until golden and crispy. Remove from the oven, discard the cocktail sticks and transfer the pears to small plates. Garnish the top of each pear with curly parsley sprigs and serve immediately.

NOTE: The pears should be fully encased by the bacon rashers, so you may need 4 rather than 3, depending on the size of your pears and your bacon rashers.

ROASTED APRICOTS WITH FETA

This effortless, elegant starter pairs creamy feta with caramelized apricots gently infused with vanilla and sugar, finished with a scattering of crunchy pistachios and a touch of fragrant mint, for a harmonious blend of sweet and savoury flavours. Ready in minutes, this amuse-bouche is one of the most popular among my guests. Try it and set the perfect tone for your dinner party.

SERVES 4

200g (7oz) block of feta cheese
6–8 apricots, halved and stoned
100ml (3½fl oz) water
1 teaspoon sugar
1 vanilla pod, split
30g (1oz) shelled pistachio nuts, chopped
4 mint leaves, to garnish

Cut the feta block in half horizontally through the thinnest dimension, like you're slicing a cake for layering. Then cut each half in half to obtain 4 rectangular pieces. Set aside.

Arrange the apricot halves, cut-side up, in a small ovenproof dish, just large enough to hold them.

Put the measured water, sugar and vanilla pod into a small saucepan. Heat until the mixture just comes to the boil, stirring to dissolve the sugar. Remove from the heat and pour over the apricots. Leave to infuse while preheating the oven to 200°C, 180°C fan (400°F), Gas Mark 6.

Roast the apricots for 10–15 minutes until tender. Remove from the oven and leave to cool until warm.

To serve, put each piece of feta on a serving plate and top with a warm apricot half. Drizzle each with some of the roasting juices, sprinkle with a quarter of the pistachios and garnish with a mint leaf. Serve the additional apricot halves and any remaining juice in a small dish alongside.

CHEESE SOUFFLÉ

This dish brings back many memories of my grandmother's kitchen. I remember beating egg whites by hand with her old-school spring-coil whisk, and I loved the moment when I could turn the bowl upside down to prove that the whites were stiff enough to fold into the béchamel. My grandmother called this her savoury cheesecake, and watching it puff up golden in the oven was such a delight. Treat yourself and make this; it's so easy, you'll want to make soufflés more often.

MAKES ENOUGH FOR 4 × 300ML (10FL OZ) BOWLS

30g (1oz) Parmesan cheese, grated
300ml (10fl oz) whole milk
4 bay leaves
5 allspice berries
pinch of ground nutmeg
2 garlic cloves, crushed
50g (1¾oz) butter, plus extra, softened, for greasing
50g (1¾oz) plain flour
pinch of fine salt
5 eggs, separated
60g (2¼oz) Comté cheese, grated, plus extra for topping

Preheat the oven to 200°C, 180°C fan (400°F), Gas Mark 6. Generously grease 4 x 300ml (10fl oz) heatproof bowls or ramekins with softened butter and coat up to the inner rim with the Parmesan.

Put the milk, bay leaves, allspice berries, nutmeg and garlic into a saucepan. Bring to a simmer, then remove from the heat and leave to infuse for 15 minutes.

Melt the butter in a medium saucepan over a medium–low heat. Add the flour and salt and stir vigorously with a spatula until fully incorporated. Strain the infused milk through a sieve into the pan, then remove from the heat. Whisk well for 1–2 minutes until you have a thick, creamy béchamel. Set aside.

Whisk the egg whites in a large mixing bowl until light, firm and glossy but not overly stiff. Fold the egg yolks and Comté into the béchamel, then gently fold in one-third of the whisked egg whites until almost incorporated. Finally, fold in the remaining egg whites until well combined.

Fill each prepared bowl or ramekin three-quarters full with the soufflé mixture and sprinkle extra grated Comté over the tops.

Place on the middle shelf in the oven and bake for 20–25 minutes, without opening the oven door, until puffed and golden on top. Serve immediately.

EGG MAYO 3 WAYS

Growing up, breakfast often meant one thing: a mountain of scrambled eggs from my grandmother's beloved hens, or the most wonderful egg salad you've ever tasted, piled high on thick slices of toasted bread, which set us up nicely for the day. This recipe is endlessly versatile for serving at any time, so whether you're going classic with an open-face sandwich or feeling fancy with a buttery flaky pastry, you can't go wrong. It's Polish fast food at its finest, with a few modern tweaks.

EACH SERVES 2

BASE RECIPE

4 hard-boiled eggs, shelled and finely chopped
3–4 tablespoons good-quality mayonnaise (see page 204 for homemade)
fine salt and freshly ground black pepper

Put the eggs and mayonnaise into a mixing bowl. Season to taste, then mix together well.

Taste and adjust the seasoning if necessary.

FOR PARMESAN EGG MAYO

50g (1¾oz) Parmesan cheese, grated, plus extra shavings to serve

To the base recipe, add the Parmesan and mix together.

Serve topped with Parmesan shavings.

FOR PICKLED RADISH EGG MAYO

1 teaspoon Pickled Radishes pickling brine (see page 214), or to taste, plus Pickled Radish slices, to garnish

To the base recipe, add the radish pickling brine and mix together.

Taste and add more as desired.

Serve garnished with pickled radish slices.

FOR LEMON HERB EGG MAYO

juice of 1 lemon
a few sprigs each of dill and parsley, roughly chopped, plus extra dill sprigs to garnish

To the base recipe, add half the lemon juice and the herbs and mix together.

Taste and add more lemon juice and seasoning as desired.

Serve garnished with dill sprigs.

RED PEPPER & BUCKWHEAT PARCELS

Good cooking doesn't always have to be complicated. Sometimes, all you need are sweet pepper gems filled with chewy, nutty buckwheat, secured with kitchen string tied in little bows. I like to serve these as is, as a starter, but if you want to make this more of a plateful, add some dressed mixed salad leaves, or serve on a layer of Greek yogurt and top the peppers with sauerkraut. You could also use them as a replacement for the ubiquitous potato alongside a roast chicken.

SERVES 4

- 150g (5½oz) toasted buckwheat (*kasha*)
- extra virgin olive oil or vegetable oil, for cooking, plus extra to serve
- 1 small onion, finely chopped
- 1 small bunch of flat leaf parsley, chopped
- 4 red Romano peppers
- salt and freshly ground black pepper

Put the buckwheat into a medium saucepan and add cold water to cover generously. Bring to the boil and season with salt, then reduce the heat and simmer gently for about 15 minutes until tender. Drain and set aside.

Preheat the oven to 200°C, 180°C fan (400°F), Gas Mark 6. Line a baking tray with nonstick baking paper.

Heat a glug of oil in a frying pan, add the onion and cook over a low heat for 5–8 minutes, or until golden brown. Season with salt and pepper, then stir in the buckwheat and cook for 5 minutes. Taste and adjust the seasoning. Stir in half the parsley, then set aside.

Cut a lengthways slit in each pepper without slicing completely in half, keeping the stalk end intact, and scrape out the seeds.

Using a small spoon, fill the opening in the peppers with the buckwheat mixture until they are generously filled. Secure by tying loosely at either end with kitchen string.

Arrange the filled peppers on the lined tray, drizzle over a generous glug of oil and season lightly with salt and pepper. Roast for 15–20 minutes until the peppers just begin to wrinkle and char.

Remove from the oven and transfer to a platter or plates. Drizzle over more oil and sprinkle with the remaining parsley before serving.

POTATO PANCAKES
PLACKI ZIEMNIACZNE

I must have eaten tonnes of these throughout my childhood, and honestly, I'd do it all over again. Although fried, these aren't heavy at all, unless you count heavenly as heavy, in which case they absolutely are. Light and crispy on the outside and tender within, they tend to disappear almost as fast as they are made.

SERVES 4

1kg (2lb 4oz) all-rounder potatoes
1 onion, grated
2 eggs, beaten
3 tablespoons plain flour
1 tablespoon salt
1 teaspoon freshly ground black pepper, plus extra to serve
vegetable oil, for cooking

TO SERVE
smoked salmon
soured cream
capers
chopped chives
thinly sliced onion
dill sprigs

Peel the potatoes, then grate into a large mixing bowl. Working in batches, put spoonfuls of the grated potato into a fine-mesh sieve set over a bowl and push down with a wooden spoon to extract as much liquid as possible, reserving it in the bowl. Alternatively, use your hands to squeeze out the excess liquid, or wrap in a clean tea towel and twist to ring it out.

Put the dry grated potato into a mixing bowl. Add the onion, eggs, flour, salt and pepper and mix together well. Stir in 1 tablespoon of the reserved potato liquid.

Line 1 or 2 large plates with kitchen paper. Heat a thin layer of oil in a heavy-based frying pan, and when hot, carefully add large spoonfuls of the potato mixture to the oil, in batches of 3 or 4, to avoid overcrowding the pan. Keeping the mounds as round as possible, push down gently with the spoon to flatten into pancake shapes. Then working with one at a time, tidy up the edges of the pancakes with the back of the spoon.

Fry over a medium heat until a deep golden brown, then turn and fry the other side. Transfer to the lined plate or plates to absorb the excess oil. Repeat until all the potato mixture has been cooked.

Serve hot topped with smoked salmon and soured cream and a good grinding of pepper, sprinkled with capers, chopped chives, thinly sliced onion and dill sprigs.

POTATO PESTO BABKA

The inspiration for this recipe comes from my grandmother's genius at turning leftover baked potatoes into the most wonderful savoury babka. It's not exactly traditional, but the twisting creates something truly special, somewhere between a bread and a pastry that's absolutely addictive. She made this with her homemade wild garlic pesto, but shop-bought basil pesto works beautifully, too.

MAKES A 900G (2LB) LOAF

- 2 potatoes, peeled (about 200g/7oz), cut into evenly sized chunks
- 150ml (5fl oz) whole milk
- 7g (¼oz) sachet fast-action dried yeast
- 2 tablespoons sugar
- 350g (12oz) strong white bread flour, plus cxtra for dusting
- 2 tablespoons extra virgin olive oil
- 1 teaspoon salt
- 190g (6¾oz) basil pesto
- 3 tablespoons finely grated Parmesan cheese
- 1 tablespoon finely grated Comté cheese

TO GARNISH (optional)
- soured cream
- chopped spring onion
- chopped chives

Cook the potatoes in a saucepan of lightly salted boiling water for 15–20 minutes until tender. Drain and mash, then set aside.

Gently warm the milk in a saucepan or in a microwavable bowl in a microwave. Transfer the milk to a large mixing bowl, add the yeast and 1 teaspoon of the sugar and whisk together with a fork. Leave to stand for 5–10 minutes, or until you see little bubbles on the surface.

Sift in the flour and add the mashed potato, oil, salt and remaining sugar. Using your hands, mix to a rough dough in the bowl, then turn out on a clean work surface. Continue kneading vigorously for about 5 minutes until you have a smooth dough.

Form the dough into a ball on the work surface, cover with the upturned mixing bowl and leave to rise for about 1 hour until doubled in size.

Line a 900g (2lb) tin with nonstick baking paper.

Roll out the dough on a lightly floured work surface into a rectangle about 30 x 25cm (12 x 10 inches). Spread over the pesto in an even layer, followed by 2 tablespoons of the Parmesan.

Starting from one long side, roll the dough up tightly into a log to enclose the filling. Using a sharp knife, cut the roll lengthways in half almost to the end, but not quite, so that you have 2 strands and the filling is exposed. Twist the strands together by folding one over the other. Transfer to the lined tin, tucking the ends in gently. Cover loosely with a clean damp tea towel and leave to prove in a warm place for 50 minutes–1 hour.

Preheat the oven to 200°C, 180°C fan (400°F), Gas Mark 6.

Sprinkle the remaining grated cheeses over the top of the dough and bake for 20 minutes. Cover the top with foil to prevent over-browning, then continue baking for another 10–15 minutes until a skewer inserted into the centre comes out clean. Remove from the oven and leave to cool completely in the tin. Serve at room temperature with the garnishes, if you like.

LEEKS WITH BEETROOT HORSERADISH

A well-boiled leek or two was a common element in my grandmother's kitchen, as these were used to add flavour to many a bouillon. My father enjoyed them as a snack with horseradish and a hard-boiled egg, as in this recipe, though I prefer Polish beetroot horseradish for its vibrant colour and extra flavour. This is a perfect starter or light lunch, served as tartines or as a sharing plate.

SERVES 4

8–12 baby leeks, cleaned
290g (10¼oz) Polish beetroot horseradish
2 tablespoons Greek yogurt
extra virgin olive oil, for drizzling
salt and freshly ground black pepper

TO SERVE (optional)
toasted bread slices
1–2 spring onions, sliced
2 hard-boiled eggs, shelled and halved

Trim the leeks to about equal length. Bring some salted water to the boil in a shallow pan large enough to hold the leeks. Add the leeks – they should be just covered by the water – and simmer gently for 5–10 minutes until tender. Remove immediately to a tray filled with iced water to keep them green, then drain on kitchen paper. Leave to cool.

Meanwhile, mix the beetroot horseradish with the yogurt. Spread on a platter or toasted bread slices as desired.

Slice the cooled leeks lengthways and arrange on the beetroot horseradish, then drizzle with extra virgin olive oil. Scatter with the spring onion or top each serving with a hard-boiled egg half and season with salt and pepper. Serve at room temperature.

CHAPTER 2

SOUPS

HOT BORSCHT
BARSZCZ CZERWONY

This quintessentially Polish soup is all about late autumn and winter, when beetroots are at their sweetest. The secret to achieving the right flavour is balancing those sweet beets with a splash of vinegar and the gentle heat of allspice. Serve it the traditional Polish way, with a slice of wholemeal bread, or with mashed potatoes in the bowl to soak up all that gorgeous ruby broth.

SERVES 4

- 1.5 litres (2¾ pints) Polish Vegetable Bouillon (see page 216), or vegetable or chicken stock
- 400g (14oz) beetroot, peeled and chopped
- 1 tablespoon sugar
- 1 teaspoon ground allspice
- 4 bay leaves
- 2 tablespoons cider vinegar
- 2 tablespoons cornflour
- salt and freshly ground black pepper
- dill sprigs, to garnish
- soured cream, to serve

Bring the bouillon or stock to a simmer in a large saucepan.

Add the beetroot, sugar, allspice, bay leaves and 1 tablespoon of the vinegar, cover the pan with a lid and simmer gently for 30–40 minutes until the beetroot is cooked through and tender.

Remove the bay leaves. Using a stick blender, blitz the soup until velvety smooth. Taste and adjust the seasoning with salt and pepper.

Transfer 2 ladlefuls of the hot soup to a small bowl. Add the cornflour and whisk to blend thoroughly. Add the cornflour mixture to the soup and simmer, stirring, until it begins to thicken.

Stir in the remaining vinegar and leave to stand for 10 minutes before tasting and adjusting the seasoning again as desired.

Serve hot, topped with a dollop of soured cream and a grinding of pepper, garnished with dill sprigs.

COLD BEETROOT & YOGURT SOUP
CHŁODNIK

Cold soup is a staple of the Polish summer kitchen, and I can hardly remember a childhood summer without this pink elixir. My grandmother never used a mandoline, but I like the elegant look of paper-thin slices in creamy fuchsia broth. Precooked beetroot are fine here; it should be hot weather when you make this, so keep yourself and your guests cool by not heating up the kitchen! You will need to season well to taste, and serve with extra lemon wedges and some hot sauce to keep this on trend for the modern palate.

SERVES 4–6

2 cooked beetroot, about 350g (12oz) total weight
1 small cucumber, about 200g (7oz), peeled
100g (3½oz) radishes
500ml (18fl oz) kefir
4 tablespoons Greek yogurt
1 small bunch of dill, chopped
1 small bunch of chives, chopped
juice of ½ lemon, or more to taste
Tabasco sauce, to taste (optional)
1 soft-boiled egg per person, shelled and halved
salt and freshly ground black pepper

Using a mandoline, slice the cooked beetroot, cucumber and radishes thinly. Alternatively, use a sharp knife to finely slice all the vegetables.

Put all the vegetables into a large mixing bowl, add the kefir, yogurt, two-thirds each of the dill and chives and ½ teaspoon salt and stir well. Cover and refrigerate for 1–2 hours to allow the flavours to blend.

Before serving, stir in the lemon juice. Taste and adjust the seasoning, adding more of anything that seems necessary and Tabasco sauce if desired.

Ladle into bowls and place an egg half in each. Divide the remaining herbs between the bowls, add a good grinding of pepper and serve.

POLISH RYE SOURDOUGH SOUP
ŻUREK

When I long for the taste of home, this more than anything is what I crave. The sourdough adds an unmistakable tang to this meaty soup, and if you have never tasted it, please do try it. It improves on standing, so it's ideal for making in advance and reheating. If this quantity is more than you need, it freezes well.

SERVES 6

1 large onion, halved
2 litres (3½ pints) Polish Vegetable Bouillon (see page 216), or vegetable or chicken stock
2 carrots, peeled and sliced into rounds
3 garlic cloves, crushed
4 bay leaves
6 allspice berries
3 tablespoons dried marjoram
10g (½oz) dried porcini mushrooms
1 apple, halved
1 tablespoon vegetable oil
250g (9oz) Polish smoked slab bacon, thickly sliced
130g (4½oz) Polish smoked sausage (*kielbasa*), coarsely chopped
500ml (18fl oz) rye sourdough starter (see Note)
2 tablespoons double cream
curly parsley sprigs, to garnish
3 soft-boiled eggs, shelled and halved, to serve

Place the onion halves, cut-side down, over a gas flame and char until aromatic and lightly blackened. If you don't have a gas hob, char in a dry griddle pan or cast-iron frying pan over a high heat.

Put the bouillon or stock, carrots, garlic, bay leaves, allspice berries, marjoram, dried mushrooms, charred onion and apple into a large saucepan. Cover with a lid and simmer gently over a low heat while you prepare the meats.

Heat the oil in a frying pan and cook the bacon over a medium–low heat, stirring, for a few minutes until golden brown. Transfer to the simmering soup. Add the sausage to the same pan and cook for 5–8 minutes until browned, then transfer to the soup. Continue simmering the soup for 20 minutes.

Stir in the rye sourdough starter and cook for 2–3 minutes until the soup begins to thicken.

To serve, remove the onion and apple halves. Ladle the soup into bowls, dividing the meats and carrots, and stir a teaspoon of cream into each serving. Top each with a soft-boiled egg half and garnish with a curly parsley sprig.

NOTE: Ready-made rye sourdough starter for the soup is available in most Polish food shops.

YOUNG BEETROOT & SPRING VEGETABLE SOUP BOTWINKA

The name tells the story; *botwinka* means young beetroot with its stalks and leaves, which is what differentiates this soup from borscht (see page 43). My version, with parsnip, is a departure from tradition. Parsley root is an everyday ingredient in Poland, often used in this recipe, and it looks like a parsnip. In the early days of cooking outside of Poland, I mistook parsnip for parsley root and attributed the different flavour to a different context. Fast forward to a wiser me, but I maintain the parsnip habit because I quite like the taste in this springtime classic.

SERVES 4–6

4 young beetroot, with stalks and leaves
200g (7oz) small new potatoes
150g (5½oz) young carrots, peeled
1 small parsnip (about 140g/5oz), peeled
1.5 litres (2¾ pints) Polish Vegetable Bouillon (see page 216), or vegetable or chicken stock
20g (¾oz) dill
juice of 1 lemon
salt and freshly ground black pepper
soured cream, to serve

Chop all the vegetables into bite-sized pieces but keep the potatoes whole if they are very small. Chop the beetroot stalks and leaves as well.

Bring the bouillon or stock to the boil in a saucepan. Season lightly with salt and pepper, add the chopped vegetables and simmer gently for about 15 minutes until just tender.

Add half the dill, taste and adjust the seasoning and simmer for another 10 minutes.

Stir in about 1 tablespoon of the lemon juice, then taste and add more, if desired, or put on the table for your guests to help themselves.

Ladle the soup into bowls and top with the remaining dill and a dollop of soured cream.

STAUB

SAUERKRAUT SOUP
KAPUŚNIAK

Is this a soup or is it a stew? It's a fine line, but like all soupy stewy dishes it develops even more flavour when refrigerated overnight and reheated the following day. Smoked ribs are a Polish staple, but if you can't find them, there are enough smoked meats here to keep the flavour going, so you could substitute spareribs or simply omit.

SERVES 4–6

500g (1lb 2oz) sauerkraut with its brine
1 litre (1¾ pints) water
6 allspice berries or 1 teaspoon ground allspice
4 bay leaves
1 tablespoon dried marjoram
100g (3½oz) smoked bacon lardons
150g (5½oz) Polish smoked or fresh sausage, cut into pieces
4–6 smoked pork ribs (optional)
1 onion, thinly sliced
vegetable oil, if needed
125g (4½oz) celeriac, peeled and grated
2 carrots, peeled and grated
1 litre (1¾ pints) Polish Vegetable Bouillon (see page 216), or vegetable or chicken stock
500g (1lb 2oz) potatoes, peeled and cut into small cubes
salt and freshly ground black pepper
curly parsley sprigs, to garnish
crusty bread, to serve

Put the sauerkraut with its brine and the measured water into a saucepan. Add the allspice, bay leaves and marjoram, cover the pan with a lid and simmer over a medium heat for about 30 minutes.

Meanwhile, heat a large saucepan over a medium heat, add the lardons, sausage and pork ribs, if using, and cook, stirring, for 3–5 minutes until aromatic and browned. Remove the meats with a slotted spoon. Set aside.

Add the onion to the meat pan and cook for 3–5 minutes until translucent, adding a little oil if necessary. Stir in the grated celeriac and carrots and cook for 3–5 minutes until all the vegetables have softened.

Pour in the bouillon or stock and return the meats to the pan, then stir in the potatoes. Cover the pan with a lid and simmer for 20 minutes.

Stir in the cooked sauerkraut along with its cooking liquid and simmer gently for another 10 minutes.

Taste and adjust the seasoning with salt and pepper. Remove the bay leaves and leave to stand for at least 1 hour before reheating and serving hot, garnished with curly parsley sprigs and accompanied with crusty bread. However, this is always better cooled, covered and refrigerated overnight, then reheated to serve the next day.

CHICKEN BARLEY SOUP
KRUPNIK

Barley, much like buckwheat, is one of those humble ingredients at the heart of Polish cooking. This substantial soup is traditionally a meat-heavy affair, and both sides of my family certainly made it that way. But my mum preferred to simmer hers with just chicken for a more subtle flavour, letting the vegetables and barley shine in the golden, turmeric-tinted broth. That's how I prefer this; it's like a gentle, warming hug on a cold day.

SERVES 6

2 litres (3½ pints) Polish Vegetable Bouillon (see page 216), or chicken or vegetable stock
3 bone-in chicken legs
4 bay leaves
6 allspice berries
175g (6oz) pearl barley
1 onion, chopped
2 carrots, peeled and sliced
1 small parsnip, peeled and sliced
1 leek, white part only, trimmed, cleaned and sliced
¼ celeriac, peeled and cut into small cubes
1 large potato, peeled and cut into small cubes
½ teaspoon ground turmeric
salt and freshly ground black pepper
dill sprigs, to garnish
crusty bread, to serve

Put the stock or bouillon, chicken, bay leaves and allspice berries into a large saucepan. Bring to the boil, then reduce the heat, cover the pan with a lid and simmer for about 45 minutes until the chicken is cooked and easy to shred.

Meanwhile, cook the pearl barley according to the packet instructions. Drain and set aside.

Remove the cooked chicken from the broth and, once cool enough to handle, shred the meat, discarding the skin. Set aside.

Taste the broth and adjust the seasoning with salt and pepper. Add all the vegetables, re-cover and simmer gently for 30–40 minutes until they are tender. Stir in the turmeric, then taste and adjust the seasoning again as desired.

Divide the cooked barley and shredded chicken between soup bowls. Ladle over the vegetables and hot broth. Garnish with dill sprigs and serve with crusty bread.

NOTE: Barley swells when left in broth, so store the grain and soup separately if there are leftovers.

POLISH RAMEN WITH PORK BELLY

My grandmother often made a bone broth, which has led me to this Polish version of ramen. I add cinnamon and pear for unexpected umami depth, plus lots of other goodies. You need to make this at least one day in advance, and the beauty is you can freeze the broth so that it's ready exactly when you need it most. This is what I crave when the weather turns or when I feel the first scratchy signs of a cold. The aromas of this soup as it simmers fill the house with their comforting warmth. Try it and you'll see.

SERVES 4

1 head of garlic, halved horizontally
½ cinnamon stick
5g (⅛oz) sachet dashi stock powder
1 pear, halved
300g (10½oz) pork belly, cut into bite-sized pieces
1 teaspoon smoked salt
400g (14oz) fresh ramen noodles

FOR THE BROTH
1.5 litres (2¾ pints) ready-made chicken and beef bone broth
1 small parsnip, peeled and roughly chopped
¼ small celeriac, peeled and roughly chopped
2 carrots, peeled
8 dried shiitake mushrooms
4 bay leaves
4 allspice berries, toasted
1 teaspoon black peppercorns
salt and freshly ground black pepper

TO SERVE
2 soft-boiled eggs, shelled and halved
furikake seasoning

Preheat the oven to 200°C, 180°C fan (400°F), Gas Mark 6.

Wrap the garlic in foil and roast on the oven shelf for about 30 minutes until tender. Remove from the oven and leave until cool enough to handle.

Meanwhile, put all the broth ingredients into a large saucepan. Bring to the boil, then reduce the heat, cover with a lid and simmer gently for 30 minutes.

Add the cinnamon, dashi and pear to the broth, then squeeze in the roasted garlic cloves from their skins. Re-cover and continue simmering for 1 hour. Remove from the heat and leave to cool, then cover and refrigerate overnight.

The next day, reheat the broth and strain, reserving the mushrooms. Taste and adjust the seasoning with salt and pepper.

Heat a small frying pan, add the pork belly pieces and cook over a medium–high heat for a few minutes, or until well browned all over. Sprinkle with the smoked salt.

Cook the ramen according to the packet instructions, then drain and divide between 4 soup bowls, along with the pork belly and mushrooms. Add a soft-boiled egg half to each. Pour in the hot broth and sprinkle with furikake seasoning. Serve immediately.

ONION SOUP WITH PEAR & PORCINI

My grandmother called this 'a constant stir soup' for good reason. Yes, you'll be stirring, but the reward is absolutely worth it. It's one of those recipes that transforms humble onions into pure deliciousness, as the caramelization brings out their sugars and using a variety of different types, plus leeks, helps deepen the flavour. This is further enhanced by the subtle umami of dried mushrooms and Grandma's secret ingredient: a pear. The best way to enjoy this soup is to make it at least one day in advance so that the flavours have time to mingle in the pot.

SERVES 6–8

55g (2oz) dried porcini mushrooms
600ml (20fl oz) boiling water
70g (2½oz) salted butter
1.5kg (3lb 5oz) onions (a mix of white, brown and pink Roscoff works well), thickly sliced
4 bay leaves
1 leek, trimmed, cleaned and thinly sliced
1 small pear, peeled, cored and grated
20g (¾oz) plain flour
1 teaspoon dried thyme or leaves from 5 thyme sprigs
300ml (10fl oz) white wine
2 litres (3½ pints) good-quality unsalted beef stock
salt and freshly ground black pepper

TO SERVE
stale sourdough or fresh baguette, enough for 6–8 slices
your favourite cheese, grated (I use Comté)

Put the dried mushrooms into a heatproof bowl, pour over the measured boiling water and soak for at least 2 hours.

Melt the butter in a heavy-based pan over a medium heat. Add the onions, cover the pan with a lid and cook for 10 minutes, stirring occasionally.

Stir in 1 teaspoon each of salt and pepper, along with the bay leaves, re-cover and cook for another 10 minutes, stirring occasionally. Remove the lid and continue cooking for 10–15 minutes until the onions begin to turn golden, stirring occasionally.

Stir in the leek and pear, re-cover and cook for about 20 minutes, stirring occasionally.

Meanwhile, strain the mushrooms, reserving the soaking liquid, then chop finely. Set aside.

Remove the lid and continue cooking, stirring, for 5–10 minutes until the onions become dark brown.

Add the flour and thyme and stir well to incorporate evenly. Cook, stirring, for 1 minute, then add the wine and chopped mushrooms. Once the wine has mostly evaporated, gradually pour in the stock, stirring gently and scraping the bottom of the pan. Add the reserved mushroom soaking liquid, re-cover and simmer for 40 minutes until the soup has thickened. Taste and adjust the seasoning. (Up to this point, the soup can be made ahead, then cooled, covered and refrigerated for 1–2 days.)

When ready to serve, preheat the oven to 200°C, 180°C fan (400°F), Gas Mark 6.

Transfer the soup to an ovenproof dish and arrange the bread slices on top. Sprinkle generously with cheese and bake for 10–20 minutes until the cheese is golden and bubbling. Serve immediately.

FRESH CHANTERELLE SOUP
ZUPA Z KURKOWA

Some of my fondest childhood memories are of early morning mushroom-hunting trips in the forest with my grandparents. The thought of that evening's delicious soup and the next morning's scrambled eggs with chanterelles made every early wake-up worth it. In Poland, the chanterelle season runs from June to October, and their subtle, earthy flavour brings all the warmth of those pleasant months straight to your plate.

SERVES 4

50g (1¾oz) unsalted butter
200g (7oz) chanterelle mushrooms, cleaned (see Note) and roughly chopped
1 small onion, finely chopped
2 garlic cloves, crushed
1.5 litres (2¾ pints) Polish Vegetable Bouillon (see page 216), or vegetable or chicken stock
2 carrots, peeled and chopped
1 parsnip, peeled and chopped
400g (14oz) small new potatoes, scrubbed and quartered
handful of chopped dill
fine salt and freshly ground black pepper
soured cream, to serve

Melt the butter in a heavy-based pan over a medium heat. Add the mushrooms, onion and garlic, cover the pan with a lid and cook for 10 minutes.

Pour in the bouillon or stock and stir gently, scraping the bottom of the pan. Taste and adjust the seasoning with salt and pepper. Add the remaining vegetables, re-cover and simmer gently for 20–30 minutes until cooked. Taste and adjust the seasoning again, then stir in the dill.

To serve, stir a generous spoonful of soured cream into the soup before ladling into bowls, or let your guests help themselves at the table.

NOTE: To clean the chanterelles, put them in a large sieve and add a handful of flour. Shake vigorously to dislodge any dirt, then rinse well. Transfer to a clean tea towel or kitchen paper and pat dry gently.

FESTIVE MUSHROOM SOUP

The moment the scent of simmering mushrooms wafts through the kitchen, I'm transported to Christmas Eves past and the child waiting impatiently for that first spoonful of what was always the opening act of our 12-course feast. My family would make this soup the day before, letting the flavours deepen overnight, and it was the dish that signalled that the celebrations had truly begun. It is mild yet flavoursome with a kind of subtle deliciousness that makes sense once you've tasted it yourself.

SERVES 6

40g (1½oz) dried porcini mushrooms
1 litre (1¾ pints) boiling water
3 small onions, halved
1 litre (1¾ pints) Polish Vegetable Bouillon (see page 216), or vegetable or chicken stock
3 bay leaves
4 allspice berries
3 carrots, peeled and halved
1 garlic clove, crushed
1 apple, halved
1 tablespoon cornflour
2 teaspoons white miso paste
400g (14oz) fresh egg noodles
4 teaspoons double cream
fine salt and freshly ground black pepper
flat leaf parsley sprigs, to garnish
crème fraîche, to serve

Put the dried mushrooms into a heatproof bowl, pour over the measured boiling water and leave to soak for at least 2 hours.

Place the onion halves, cut-side down, over a gas flame and char until aromatic and lightly blackened. If you don't have a gas hob, char in a dry griddle pan or cast-iron frying pan over a high heat.

Put the bouillon or stock, bay leaves, allspice berries, charred onion, carrots, garlic and apple into a large saucepan. Bring just to the boil, then reduce the heat to a simmer. Add the mushrooms along with their soaking liquid and continue to simmer for 30 minutes.

Mix the cornflour and miso paste with a few ladelfuls of the hot soup in a small bowl to create a smooth mixture. Gently stir into the soup and simmer, stirring, until thickened.

Cook the noodles according to the packet instructions, then drain.

Taste the soup and adjust the seasoning with salt and pepper, then discard the apple. Stir in the cream and noodles. Ladle the hot soup into bowls and top with a dollop of crème fraîche, then garnish with a flat leaf parsley sprig and serve immediately.

PICKLED CUCUMBER SOUP
ZUPA OGÓRKOWA

This is the quickest path to a crowd-pleasing soup I know, and my foreign friends are always surprised by how much they love this traditional dish with its unusual name. In Poland, it's commonly made with chicken stock but it's equally delicious with a vegetable stock, letting the sweet vegetables and sour cucumbers really shine through. The crucial thing is to use Polish pickled cucumber in brine, not vinegar. You want those sour pickles, not the sweet kind, for the specific tangy flavour that makes this soup so special.

SERVES 6

2 litres (3½ pints) Polish Vegetable Bouillon (see page 216), or vegetable or chicken stock
4 bay leaves
4 allspice berries
3 garlic cloves, crushed
1 leek, green part only, trimmed, cleaned, halved and thinly sliced
2 carrots, peeled and grated
1 small parsnip, peeled and grated
1 onion, peeled and grated
300g (10½oz) potatoes (any all-rounder variety)
400g (14oz) Polish pickled cucumbers in vinegar (*konserwowe*; see page 205 for homemade)
3 tablespoons double cream
salt and freshly ground black pepper
dill sprigs, to garnish

Pour the bouillon or stock into a large saucepan and bring to a simmer over a low heat. Add the bay leaves, allspice berries, garlic, leek, carrots, parsnip and onion, cover the pan with a lid and simmer gently while you prepare the potatoes.

Peel the potatoes, then coarsely grate, adding them to the simmering stock as you go to keep them from browning. Re-cover and simmer for 30 minutes. Taste and adjust the seasoning with salt and pepper.

Coarsely grate the pickled cucumbers and add to the soup, then re-cover and simmer for another 15 minutes.

Serve hot, each serving topped with cream and garnished with a dill sprig.

POTATO VELOUTÉ
KARTOFLANKA

This simple potato soup, essentially just blended potato, garlic and shallot, is a recipe from my grandmother's youth and yet my bistro diners are always amazed by its flavour. I love how this soup bridges our generations. While Grandma's version went classic with a finishing touch of crispy bacon lardons, I have transformed it into something unexpectedly elegant and contemporary with the addition of kimchi floating on the surface, along with soured cream.

SERVES 6

40g (1½oz) unsalted butter
2 shallots, finely chopped
3 garlic cloves, very finely chopped
1kg (2lb 4oz) all-rounder potatoes, peeled and finely chopped
1 litre (1¾ pints) Polish Vegetable Bouillon (see page 216), or vegetable or chicken stock
3 bay leaves
¼ teaspoon ground allspice
50ml (2fl oz) double cream, or more if desired
salt and freshly ground black pepper
dill sprigs, to garnish

TO SERVE
kimchi
soured cream

Melt 25g (1oz) of the butter in a heavy-based pan, add the shallots and cook over a medium heat for about 3 minutes until translucent. Add the garlic, potatoes and remaining butter and cook, stirring, for 1 minute.

Add the bouillon or stock, bay leaves and allspice and bring to a simmer. Taste and adjust the seasoning with salt and pepper. Cover the pan with a lid and cook over a low heat for about 30 minutes until the potatoes are tender.

Remove the bay leaves and stir in the double cream. Using a stick blender, blitz until velvety smooth, adding more cream for a thinner texture if desired. Taste and adjust the seasoning as desired.

Serve hot in bowls topped with kimchi and soured cream, with a good grinding of pepper, garnished with dill sprigs.

NOTE: Anchovies or smoked salmon would make an equally bold and gorgeous garnish.

TOMATO, MANGO & GINGER SOUP

If you like carrot and ginger soup, this is going to be your next favourite. I grew up on tomato soup made from my grandmother's homemade passata, but this recipe links my Polish heritage with my travels through East Asia and India, and the unexpected combination surprises my bistro guests every time! The addition of coconut cuts through the tomatoes' acidity beautifully, ginger adds warmth and mango brings just the right sweetness. Sunshine in a bowl.

SERVES 4

3 tablespoons coconut oil
1 onion, chopped
400g (14oz) can peeled plum tomatoes
20g (3/4oz) fresh root ginger, peeled and finely chopped
350g (12oz) passata
400g (14oz) can coconut milk
1/2 teaspoon fine salt, or to taste
1 ripe mango, stoned, peeled and chopped
1–2 teaspoons fish sauce (optional)
flat leaf parsley sprigs, to garnish
Greek yogurt or cream, to serve

Heat the coconut oil in a saucepan, add the onion and cook over a medium heat for about 5 minutes until translucent.

Add the tomatoes, cover the pan with a lid and simmer for 5 minutes. Using a wooden spoon, roughly mash the tomato pieces, then stir in the ginger and passata. Re-cover and simmer for another 5 minutes.

Stir in the coconut milk, re-cover and simmer for 5 minutes, then season with the salt. Cover again and simmer for a final 5 minutes.

Remove from the heat and stir in the mango. Using a stick blender, blitz the soup until velvety smooth. Taste and adjust the seasoning, adding the fish sauce to taste if desired. Swirl in a spoonful of yogurt or cream just before serving, and garnish with a flat leaf parsley sprig.

NOTE: For more spicy heat, increase the ginger and add chopped fried chilli to taste.

TOMATO & CHERRY GAZPACHO

With a cherry tree behind the house and a greenhouse full of abundant tomato plants, my resourceful grandmother created this ingenious recipe to celebrate these summer treasures. Like many cold soups traditionally enjoyed across Poland during the warm months, this transforms simple garden bounty into a refreshing ruby bowl of beauty and cheer.

SERVES 4–6

700g (1lb 9oz) ripe tomatoes, roughly chopped
200g (7oz) cucumber, peeled, deseeded and roughly chopped
150g (5½oz) cherries, pitted
3 basil leaves, plus extra sprigs to garnish
1 tablespoon tomato purée
about 3 tablespoons sherry vinegar, or to taste
1 tablespoon extra virgin olive oil, plus extra for drizzling
salt and freshly ground black pepper
small cubes of feta cheese, to garnish

Put the tomatoes, cucumber, cherries, basil, tomato purée and 2 tablespoons of the vinegar in a food processor or blender and blitz until just smooth.

Transfer to a bowl. Taste and adjust the seasoning with salt and pepper, add the remaining vinegar, then taste and add a little more if needed. Stir in the oil. Cover and refrigerate for at least 1 hour to allow the flavours to marry before serving.

To serve, ladle into bowls, then scatter with small cubes of feta, garnish with a basil sprig and drizzle over more oil.

NOTE: Try replacing the cherries with 150–180g (5½–6¼oz) ripe peaches, skinned and stoned.

CELERIAC & APPLE SOUP

When I need something to please absolutely everyone, this is the soup I choose. The way the earthy celeriac mingles with the sweetness of the apple creates a soup with such a velvety texture that even the fussiest eaters happily finish their bowls. It also has the virtue of perfect discretion; the flavours are subtle, making it a gentle introduction to a meal without stealing the spotlight from whatever you're serving as the main event. And did I mention that it is so easy to make, especially if you opt for ready-made stock.

SERVES 4

30g (1oz) butter
1 shallot, chopped
450g (1lb) celeriac, peeled and cut into small cubes
2 bay leaves
1 large apple, peeled, cored and chopped
1 garlic clove, crushed
1.2 litres (2 pints) Polish Vegetable Bouillon (see page 216), or vegetable stock
salt and freshly ground black pepper

TO SERVE
60g (2¼oz) croutons
40g (1½oz) flaked almonds, toasted
1-2 tablespoons extra virgin olive oil

Melt the butter in a heavy-based pan over a low heat, add the shallot and cook for 3–5 minutes until translucent.

Add the celeriac, bay leaves and apple and cook gently, stirring occasionally, for about 10 minutes until aromatic. Add the garlic and stir again.

Pour in the bouillon or stock and bring to a simmer. Taste and adjust the seasoning with salt and pepper. Cover the pan with a lid and simmer for 30–40 minutes until the celeriac is tender.

Remove the pan from the heat and discard the bay leaves. Using a stick blender, blitz the soup until velvety smooth. Taste and adjust the seasoning.

To serve, ladle into 4 bowls, divide the croutons and toasted flaked almonds between them and drizzle with the oil.

STAUB
COCOTTE

CHAPTER 3

MEAT & FISH

MY GRANNY'S CHICKEN SCHNITZEL

I could eat schnitzel every day and never tire of it, especially when I remember those Sunday afternoons filled with the aroma of garlic, black pepper and fresh parsley. My grandma swore by garlic and pepper, using them often, and I've carried that tradition into my own kitchen because they really do elevate meat to another level. Serve this with a slaw (see pages 141 and 146) and mashed potatoes or pickles, and don't skip the mustard and capers for that perfect tangy finish. Any leftovers make exceptional sandwiches the next day.

SERVES 4

4 skinless, boneless chicken breasts
2 tablespoons garlic granules
½ small bunch of parsley, finely chopped
100g (3½oz) plain flour
2 eggs, beaten
100g (3½oz) dried breadcrumbs
150ml (5fl oz) sunflower oil
salt and freshly ground black pepper

TO SERVE
capers
lemon wedges
Polish pickled cucumbers in vinegar (*konserwowe*; see page 205 for homemade)
mustard

Place each chicken breast between 2 sheets of baking paper and pound with a rolling pin to flatten out as thinly as possible without creating any holes.

Season each flattened chicken breast on both sides with the garlic granules, parsley and salt and pepper. Stack the seasoned chicken pieces on top of each other and refrigerate for at least 2 hours, or cover and refrigerate overnight.

When ready to cook, place 3 shallow dishes side by side on the work surface and fill one with the flour, one with the beaten egg (adding a splash of water if necessary) and one with the breadcrumbs. Then line a large plate with kitchen paper for draining.

Heat the oil in a heavy-based frying pan large enough to hold 2 chicken breasts at a time. As it heats, dip one chicken piece in the flour and tap off the excess, then dip in the egg, allowing the excess to drip off, and finally place in the breadcrumbs, pushing down to coat well on both sides. Carefully add the coated chicken to the hot oil and repeat for the second chicken piece. Cook for about 2–3 minutes on each side until deep golden and cooked through. Transfer the cooked chicken to the lined plate and repeat with the remaining chicken pieces.

Serve hot with a grinding of salt and pepper and a sprinkling of capers, with lemon wedges for squeezing over and accompanied by Polish pickled cucumbers and mustard.

POT ROAST POUSSIN WITH VANILLA & PAPRIKA

Experimentation in the kitchen led me to this vanilla and paprika combination and it has since become my favourite way to transform simple poussin into something extraordinary. The secret is using the best spices you can find: plump, fragrant vanilla pods and vibrant red paprika that denotes freshness. As the poussins roast gently in the safety of the pot, they create the most incredible juices, deeply savoury with hints of sweetness, so have thick slices of sourdough ready for mopping up every drop. If you like heat, add a pinch of cayenne to the mix.

SERVES 2

70g (2½oz) unsalted butter, softened
2 vanilla pods, split
2 poussins, about 500g (1lb 2oz) each
2 shallots, peeled but left whole
paprika, to season
fine salt and freshly ground black pepper

Preheat the oven to 200°C, 180°C fan (400°F), Gas Mark 6.

Put the butter in a small bowl. Scrape the seeds from the vanilla pods into the butter and mix well. Reserve the pods.

Smear the birds all over with about half the flavoured butter, then season with salt and pepper. Fill the cavity of each bird with a shallot, then sprinkle all over generously with paprika.

Place the poussins, breast-side down, in a large casserole dish with a tight-fitting lid, cover with the lid and roast for 20 minutes.

Remove from the oven and turn the birds over. Dust with more paprika if desired and place a vanilla pod on each. Add the remaining butter and re-cover.

Reduce the oven temperature to 180°C, 160°C fan (350°F), Gas Mark 4 and return the casserole to the oven for another 30 minutes.

Check the poussins for doneness: the juices should run clear when the thigh is pierced with a skewer. If necessary, roast for a few more minutes until cooked through. Remove from the oven and leave to rest for 10 minutes before serving.

CHICKEN MEATBALLS WITH TOMATO SAUCE & CELERIAC

Back in Poland, as the days grew shorter and autumn settled in, these meatballs would appear on our table, a delicious signal that the seasons were changing. I now pair them with tomato sauce and the subtle sweetness of celeriac that melts beautifully into both. A secret: leftover meatballs are divine on toasted sourdough with mustard and fresh herbs – perhaps even better than the original meal.

SERVES 4

FOR THE TOMATO SAUCE
1 tablespoon extra virgin olive oil
1 garlic clove, very finely chopped
3 basil leaves, plus extra to garnish
400g (14oz) can chopped tomatoes
2 anchovy fillets, finely chopped (optional)
salt and freshly ground black pepper

FOR THE MEATBALLS
500g (1lb 2oz) minced chicken
2 small garlic cloves, crushed
20g (¾oz) Comté cheese, grated
80g (3oz) breadcrumbs
1 egg
1 small bunch of parsley, finely chopped
1 tablespoon white miso
½ teaspoon fine salt
½ teaspoon freshly ground black pepper
1–2 tablespoons sunflower oil

FOR THE CELERIAC PURÉE
80g (3oz) unsalted butter
1 celeriac, peeled and cut into small cubes
2 bay leaves, plus extra to garnish
¼ teaspoon ground allspice
2 potatoes (any all-rounder variety), peeled and cut into evenly sized chunks
1 teaspoon white miso
2 tablespoons crème fraîche, or more to taste
salt and freshly ground black pepper

For the tomato sauce, heat the oil in a heavy-based pan, reduce the heat and add the garlic and basil leaves. Cook, stirring, for 30 seconds, then stir in the canned tomatoes. Cover the pan with a lid and cook for 10 minutes, stirring occasionally. Add the anchovies, if using, and season to taste with salt and pepper. Set aside.

Preheat the oven to 200°C, 180°C fan (400°F), Gas Mark 6. Line a baking tray with nonstick baking paper.

Put all the ingredients for the meatballs, except the oil, into a large mixing bowl and mix together well. Form the mixture into balls weighing about 25g (1oz) each and arrange on the lined tray. Drizzle with the oil and bake for about 20 minutes until golden brown.

Meanwhile, make the celeriac purée. Melt 50g (1¾oz) of the butter in another heavy-based pan, add the celeriac and cook for about 10 minutes until beginning to caramelize. Add water to just cover, the bay leaves, allspice and a good pinch of salt and simmer gently until tender. Drain.

Meanwhile, cook the potatoes in a saucepan of lightly salted boiling water for 15–20 minutes until tender, then drain.

Melt the remaining butter, then stir in the miso. Roughly mash together the cooked potatoes and celeriac, then stir in the miso butter and crème fraîche. Taste and adjust the seasoning with salt and pepper.

Warm the tomato sauce. Serve the meatballs with the sauce and celeriac purée, garnished with basil leaves.

SPICED BUTTER CHICKEN WITH MASH

A buttery alternative to your usual roasted chicken legs, featuring Grandma's favourite spice mix, tinted red with sweet paprika. Easy, tasty and rather regal! Potatoes simmered in stock (a cube is fine here) lend a gently infused flavour, and they help mop up that yummy spiced chicken butter. Accompany with your favourite cooked veg, mine being baby carrots.

SERVES 2

½ teaspoon fine salt
½ teaspoon coarsely ground black pepper
½ teaspoon paprika
½ teaspoon garlic granules
¼ teaspoon sugar
2 chicken legs
60g (2¼oz) unsalted butter
a cooked vegetable, such as baby carrots, to serve

FOR THE MASH
500g (1lb 2oz) all-rounder potatoes
1 litre (1¾ pints) vegetable or chicken stock
30g (1oz) butter
fine salt

For the chicken, put the salt, pepper, paprika, garlic granules and sugar into a dish large enough to hold the chicken legs and mix together well. Coat the chicken pieces on both sides with the spices, cover and leave to marinate at room temperature while you peel the potatoes and cut into evenly sized chunks for the mash.

Preheat the oven to 200°C, 180°C fan (400°F), Gas Mark 6.

Melt half the butter for the chicken in a frying pan, add the chicken pieces, skin-side down, and cook over a medium–high heat for 10–15 minutes until browned. Turn and cook the other side for 3–5 minutes just to colour.

Transfer the chicken, skin-side up, to a casserole dish with a tight-fitting lid and pour in the pan juices. Add the remaining butter. Cover with the lid and roast for 20–30 minutes, or until the juices run clear when the thigh is pierced with a skewer.

Meanwhile, put the potatoes into a saucepan, pour over the stock and bring to the boil, then reduce the heat and simmer for about 20 minutes until tender.

Drain the potatoes, reserving a few spoonfuls of stock. Mash well and stir in the butter. Taste and adjust the seasoning with salt, adding some of the reserved stock if the potatoes are very thick.

Divide the mash between 2 plates and arrange a chicken leg on top of each. Drizzle over the chicken cooking juices and serve accompanied by your cooked vegetable of choice.

OPEN-FACE CHICKEN SANDWICH

Sunday meals in Poland frequently featured roast chicken, so my grandmother's Monday meals often involved the chicken leftovers. She put sweet paprika in everything, and leftover chicken was no exception. It certainly helps to brighten up this traditional sandwich favourite, to which I've added a contemporary twist of heat in the form of gochujang, Korean red chilli paste and some green bits.

SERVES 2

25g (1oz) butter
200g (7oz) cooked chicken meat, shredded
1 teaspoon sweet or smoked paprika
½ teaspoon coarsely ground black pepper
¼ teaspoon smoked salt
1 teaspoon gochujang
2 slices of sourdough bread

TO SERVE
2 spring onions, chopped
Parmesan cheese, grated
1 avocado, halved, stoned, peeled and sliced

Melt the butter in a small frying pan, add the shredded chicken and seasonings and mix well to blend and heat through.

Meanwhile, toast the sourdough bread slices.

Divide the hot seasoned chicken between the toasted bread slices. Sprinkle over the spring onions and a dusting of Parmesan, then serve accompanied by the sliced avocado.

DUCK WITH ROASTED RHUBARB

I cannot resist the lovely pink stalks of forced rhubarb that appear in late winter. Not only are they prettier, they are sweeter and ideal for roasting as an accompaniment to rich meat such as duck. However, the pairing of duck and rhubarb works in any season, and I personally enjoy the fruit's tartness, which is why I keep the sugar to a minimum. The addition of your favourite fruity chutney adds just the right balance. This is perfect when you want a light alternative to the standard meat/potato/green veg situation.

SERVES 2

2 duck breasts, about 200g (7oz) each
1 teaspoon dried thyme
400g (14oz) rhubarb stalks
3 teaspoons sugar, or to taste
juice of 1 orange
30g (1oz) cashew nuts, roughly chopped
salt and freshly ground black pepper
apple or other fruity chutney, to serve

Pierce the skin of the duck breasts all over with a fork, then season on both sides with salt, pepper and the thyme. Leave to stand for 10 minutes.

Meanwhile, preheat the oven to 200°C, 180°C fan (400°F), Gas Mark 6. Line a baking tray with nonstick baking paper.

Cut each rhubarb stalk into thirds, or trim as needed, so that they are all approximately the same length. Arrange the rhubarb in a single layer on the lined tray, sprinkle over the sugar and set aside.

Heat a heavy-based frying pan, just big enough to hold the duck, over a medium–high heat. When hot, add the duck, skin-side down, and cook for 3–5 minutes until just brown. Turn and cook the other side for 1 minute. Transfer the duck to the tray with the rhubarb.

Deglaze the pan with the orange juice, stir for about 30 seconds, then pour over the duck.

Roast the duck and rhubarb for 15 minutes. Remove from the oven and leave the duck to rest for 5–10 minutes. Test the rhubarb for doneness; if necessary, return to the oven while the duck rests.

To serve, arrange the rhubarb on plates and top with the duck breasts. Scatter over the cashews and drizzle over any roasting juices. Serve with the chutney alongside.

ROAST DUCK LEG & APPLE

Duck was my grandfather's favourite. Growing up, it appeared on our table far more often than chicken. Duck and rabbit, too, were staples in the kitchen in those days. Duck leg was the most frequent because it had great flavour and was so easy to cook. This goes very well with the Red Cabbage & Apple Slaw on page 146.

SERVES 2

2 duck legs
1 teaspoon vegetable oil
1 head of garlic, halved horizontally
a few thyme sprigs, plus extra to garnish
2 small apples, halved and cored
salt and freshly ground black pepper
mustard, to serve

Preheat the oven to 180°C, 160°C fan (350°F), Gas Mark 4.

Pat the duck legs dry with kitchen paper, coat lightly with the oil and season with salt and pepper on both sides.

Heat a frying pan over a medium–high heat. When hot, add the duck, skin-side down, and cook for about 5 minutes until crisp and golden. Turn and cook the meat side for 3–5 minutes until browned, pushing down the edges to help the fat render.

Remove from the pan and, when cool enough to handle, trim the excess fat from the edges but leave the crispy skin in place.

Arrange the duck, skin-side down, along with the garlic, cut-sides up, and thyme, in a roasting tin just large enough to hold the ingredients, including the apples. Season lightly with salt and pepper and drizzle over the pan juices – you may need to reheat the pan to loosen them. Roast for 30 minutes.

Add the apple halves, turn the duck pieces over and roast for another 30 minutes, adding a few spoonfuls of water to the pan if it is drying out.

Serve hot, garnished with extra thyme sprigs, with mustard on the side.

GARLIC PEPPER RABBIT WITH PEAR & MISO

This is a beloved regular at the bistro and is always my first choice for date dinners at the supper club, probably because it looks impressively complex. Surprisingly, it is very easy to prepare. Rabbit is more widely available than people think – an excellent alternative to chicken at a similar price – and the way the sweet pears and miso butter play against the garlic pepper creates a spectacular taste combination that makes the dish extra special.

SERVES 2

2 rabbit legs
100g (3½oz) unsalted butter
4 teaspoons white miso
2 small just-ripe pears, peeled but kept whole with stalk intact
1 onion, halved
Little Gem lettuce salad, to serve

FOR THE GARLIC PEPPER SPICE MIX

2½ tablespoons garlic granules
2 tablespoons coarsely ground black pepper
1 tablespoon paprika
2 teaspoons fine salt
1 teaspoon caster sugar

Preheat the oven to 180°C, 160°C fan (350°F), Gas Mark 4.

Mix all the ingredients for the garlic pepper spice mix together in a small bowl.

Sprinkle the rabbit legs generously with the spice mix and set aside on a plate. (The leftover spice mix can be stored in a clean airtight jar.)

Melt the butter and miso together in a casserole dish with a tight-fitting lid, stirring to blend. When foaming, add the rabbit pieces and turn to coat well. Then arrange the rabbit, meat-side down, cover the pan with the lid and roast for 10 minutes.

Remove from the oven, add the pears and onion and baste with the sauce. Re-cover and roast for another 20 minutes.

Turn the rabbit legs over and baste with the sauce, then cover again and roast for a final 20 minutes, or until cooked through. Remove from the oven and leave the rabbit to rest in the covered pan for 5–10 minutes.

Transfer the rabbit and pears to serving plates, spoon over the pan juices and serve with a Little Gem salad on the side.

BRISKET WITH ESPRESSO & CHIPOTLE

I remember my grandmother making this brisket with ground coffee from her old percolator, filling the house with the most incredible aroma. I've updated her recipe with espresso, and the deeper, richer flavour takes it to another level. Yes, it needs four hours in the oven, but when you taste how the coffee plays with smoky chipotle and just a whisper of vanilla, you'll understand why this is the only way I make brisket now. One bite and you'll be hooked.

SERVES 4–6

- 1kg (2lb 4oz) good-quality beef brisket
- 1 tablespoon garlic salt
- 500ml (18fl oz) beef or vegetable stock
- 250ml (9fl oz) espresso
- 3 tablespoons chipotle paste
- 1 tablespoon paprika
- 1 teaspoon ground allspice
- 4 cloves
- 2 vanilla pods, split
- 2 teaspoons Dijon mustard
- 2 tablespoons dark muscovado sugar
- 1 tablespoon tomato ketchup, or to taste
- 3 tablespoons vodka (optional)
- fine salt and freshly ground black pepper
- chopped chives, to garnish
- Polish Potato Dumplings (see page 219), to serve (optional)

If the brisket is rolled, untie it so that it lies flat. Season all over with the garlic salt, cover and leave to stand at room temperature for a few minutes.

Meanwhile, preheat the oven to 180°C, 160°C fan (350°F), Gas Mark 4.

Put the stock, espresso, chipotle paste, spices, vanilla pods, mustard and sugar into a casserole dish with a tight-fitting lid just large enough to hold the beef comfortably and stir to blend. Add the beef, cut in half if necessary to fit in the pan. The liquid should come three-quarters of the way up the sides of the beef, so add water if necessary.

Cover the contents of the pan with a damp piece of nonstick baking paper to slow down evaporation, then cover with the lid. Cook for 1 hour.

Turn the beef over, re-cover with the paper and the lid and cook for another hour. Repeat the turning process but this time taste and adjust the seasoning with salt and pepper. If the liquid has evaporated too much, top up with water or stock so that it comes halfway up the sides of the meat. Cover again and cook for another hour, then repeat the turning and tasting, topping up the liquid as necessary, before cooking for a final hour.

Remove from the oven and transfer the meat to a large plate. Taste the sauce and adjust the seasoning, adding the ketchup and vodka as desired. When the meat is cool enough to handle, shred and return to the sauce.

Serve hot, garnished with chopped chives, on a bed of the potato dumplings if desired.

POLISH BEEF ROLLS
ZRAZY WOŁOWE

While Brits gather round their Sunday roast, Polish families have their own beloved tradition: these beef rolls. I can still picture them arriving at the Sunday table, alongside nutty toasted buckwheat glistening with caramelized onions, accompanied by whatever slaw was in season; cabbage in winter, cucumber in summer. It's the kind of meal that transforms a regular Sunday into something worth remembering.

SERVES 6

about 1kg (2lb 4oz) beef topside, cut into 6 x 1–1.5cm (½–5/8 inch) slices
4–6 tablespoons Dijon, brown or wholegrain mustard
3 smoked streaky bacon rashers, cut in half widthways
1 large carrot, peeled and cut lengthways into 6 pieces
2–3 Polish gherkins in vinegar, sliced
1 banana shallot, cut lengthways into 6 pieces
3 tablespoons duck or goose fat or butter
100ml (3½fl oz) red or white wine
1 small onion, finely chopped
3 garlic cloves, thinly sliced
3 bay leaves
1 sage sprig
4 thyme sprigs
1 tablespoon cornflour
3 tablespoons hot water
salt and freshly ground black pepper

Pound each beef slice with a rolling pin to even out and flatten as thinly as possible; avoid creating too many holes, but one or two are fine.

Working with one slice at a time, lay the beef flat on a clean work surface and season lightly with salt and pepper, then spread the top with the mustard. Starting at one short side, arrange one piece of bacon, topped with a piece each of carrot, gherkin and shallot, widthways. Roll the beef up tightly to enclose the filling. Secure each end firmly with kitchen string.

Heat the fat or butter in a flameproof shallow casserole dish with a lid large enough to hold the rolls comfortably over a medium–high heat. When hot, add the beef and cook for 2–3 minutes on each side until seared all over. Transfer the rolls to a clean plate.

Reduce the heat to the lowest setting and add the wine, onion and garlic, scraping the bottom of the pan to loosen any stuck-on bits. Return the rolls to the pan, arranging them in a single layer, add the herbs and pour in enough water to cover the beef halfway.

Cover the pan with the lid and simmer over a very low heat for 1½ hours. Check occasionally during cooking to make sure the liquid is not evaporating too quickly, topping up with water if necessary to keep the rolls half submerged.

Meanwhile, put the buckwheat into a large saucepan and add cold water to cover generously. Bring to the boil and season with salt, then reduce the heat and simmer gently for about 15 minutes. Drain and set aside.

Melt the butter or heat the oil in a large frying pan, add the onion and cook for about 3 minutes until translucent. Set aside in the pan.

FOR THE BUCKWHEAT

400g (14oz) toasted buckwheat (*kasha*)

15–25g (½–1oz) butter or 1–2 tablespoons vegetable oil

1 small onion, finely chopped

TO SERVE

2–3 Polish pickled cucumbers in vinegar (*konserwowe*), finely diced (see page 205 for homemade)

large handful of dill, chopped

Blend the cornflour with the measured hot water in a small bowl. Remove the beef rolls to a clean plate, then taste the sauce for seasoning and adjust as necessary. Add the cornflour mixture to the sauce and stir constantly until thickened. Return the rolls to the sauce to rewarm.

Add the buckwheat to the cooked onion and rewarm gently over a low heat for 2–3 minutes, stirring.

Meanwhile, in a small bowl, mix the diced pickles and chopped dill.

Serve the beef rolls, sliced, on a bed of the buckwheat, topped with the sauce and the dill-pickle garnish.

MY GRANNY'S GOULASH

I just loved dipping thick slices of sourdough bread into this rich, saucy goulash as soon as Grandma took it off the stove, still bubbling away in the casserole dish. Back home, Mum always served it with pearl barley and a pickled cucumber on the side. These days, in London, I've dressed it up with some smoky spices, and when serving, I alternate between crusty baguette, creamy mash or my favourite thick ribbon noodles.

SERVES 4–6

500g (1lb 2oz) chuck steak, cut into small cubes
1 teaspoon garlic salt
2–3 tablespoons sunflower oil
1 onion, halved and sliced
4 bay leaves
6 allspice berries
2 tablespoons plain flour
1 teaspoon sweet paprika
1 teaspoon smoked paprika
1 teaspoon smoked salt
1 tablespoon Dijon mustard
1 tablespoon tomato purée
500ml (18fl oz) vegetable or beef stock, or more as needed or desired
1 large carrot, peeled and sliced
250g (9oz) mushrooms, thickly sliced
3 garlic cloves, thinly sliced
1 small red pepper, cored, deseeded and sliced
salt and freshly ground black pepper
chopped chives, to garnish
400–600g (14oz–1lb 5oz) fresh thick ribbon noodles, cooked and drained, to serve

Season the meat with the garlic salt. Heat the oil in a heavy-based pan over a high heat, add the meat and sear until browned but not cooked through.

Stir in the onion, bay leaves and allspice berries. Reduce the heat, cover the pan with a lid and cook for about 5 minutes until the onion softens.

Stir in the flour, sweet paprika, smoked paprika and smoked salt and cook, stirring, for 1 minute. Then add the mustard, tomato purée and stock and stir until well blended. Re-cover and simmer very gently for 1 hour. Check to ensure the liquid does not evaporate and top up if necessary with more stock or water.

Add the carrot, mushrooms, garlic and red pepper and stir to mix. Taste and adjust the seasoning with salt and pepper, then cover again and simmer for another 20–30 minutes until the meat is tender and the vegetables are cooked.

Taste for seasoning and serve hot with the noodles, sprinkled with chopped chives to garnish.

HUNTER'S STEW
BIGOS

If one dish captures Polish autumn and Christmas, it's bigos, an iconic sauerkraut and meat stew named after November's Hubertus hunt. For me, it's pure comfort and umami heaven with complex, layered flavours. My twist is to add a pinch of red curry paste, which is a surprisingly inspired finishing touch. Bigos always tastes better the second day, so cook ahead, and if you want more tomato in it, add some ketchup when reheating. It freezes beautifully, too, so it's perfect for batch cooking.

SERVES 6–8

50g (1¾oz) dried porcini mushrooms
500ml (18fl oz) boiling water
900g (2lb) sauerkraut
5 bay leaves
3 tablespoons vegetable oil
200g (7oz) thick sliced smoked bacon, cut into bite-sized pieces, or lardons
200g (7oz) boneless pork shoulder, cut into bite-sized pieces
200g (7oz) Polish smoked sausage (*kielbasa*), cut into bite-sized pieces
1 teaspoon ground allspice
1 teaspoon freshly ground black pepper, or more to taste
50g (1¾oz) prunes, pitted and roughly chopped
4 tablespoons tomato purée
Thai red curry paste, to taste (optional)
tomato ketchup, to taste (optional)
fine salt

Put the dried mushrooms into a heatproof bowl, pour over the measured boiling water and leave to soak for at least 2 hours.

Drain the sauerkraut and rinse well. Squeeze handfuls to remove the excess vinegar, then roughly chop. Put the sauerkraut into a saucepan, add the bay leaves and pour over just enough water to cover. Cover the pan with a lid and simmer for 30 minutes, or until most of the liquid has evaporated. Keep an eye on it to ensure it doesn't evaporate too quickly.

Meanwhile, heat the oil in a large saucepan, add the meats and cook over a medium heat until they are nicely browned, stirring occasionally.

Strain the mushrooms, reserving their soaking liquid, and chop. Add the mushrooms to the meats with the allspice, pepper, prunes, tomato purée and a few spoonfuls of the reserved mushroom soaking liquid. Stir well.

Add the cooked sauerkraut and bay leaves to the meat mixture and stir well. If the mixture is dry, add more of the mushroom soaking liquid, or just water if there is none left. Taste and adjust the seasoning with salt and pepper if necessary. Leave to stand for at least a few hours before reheating to serve, adding the red curry paste and/or tomato ketchup as desired, but this is much better refrigerated and served the next day.

STAUB
STAUB

CHOU FARCI

I like to think of these as cabbage rolls' elegant cousin (see page 125); no rustic tomato sauce required. While traditionally this is made as one large dish to share, and this is how my grandmother did it using a cake tin, I prefer making individual portions at my bistro. It feels more personal, with everyone getting an equal-sized serving. Leftovers, if you have any, reheat beautifully.

MAKES 8 INDIVIDUAL CAKES OR A 22CM (8½ INCH) CAKE

1 Savoy cabbage
100g (3½oz) toasted buckwheat (*kasha*)
30g (1oz) butter, plus extra for greasing
2 tablespoons vegetable oil
1 small onion, finely chopped
2 carrots, peeled and grated
300g (10½oz) minced beef
200g (7oz) minced pork
½ teaspoon ground allspice
½ teaspoon paprika, plus extra to serve
pinch of cayenne pepper
2 garlic cloves, crushed
3–4 sun-dried tomatoes in oil, drained and finely chopped
60g (2¼oz) tomato purée
fine salt and freshly ground black pepper
dill sprigs, to garnish
crème fraîche, to serve

Bring a large saucepan of salted water to the boil. Remove the toughest outer leaves from the cabbage, then choose 16 large leaves and remove carefully. (If making a single round shape, you will need only 10–12 leaves.) Add the whole cabbage leaves to the boiling water and cook for 10–15 minutes until tender but not falling apart. Drain, then transfer to kitchen paper to absorb the excess water. If the cabbage leaves have tough cores, cut them out with a small sharp knife in a V-shape. This will make it easier to shape them in the pan.

Put the buckwheat into a separate saucepan and add cold water to cover generously. Bring to the boil and season with ½ teaspoon salt, then reduce the heat and simmer gently for about 15 minutes until tender.

Meanwhile, melt the butter with the oil in a heavy-based pan. Add the onion and carrots and cook over a medium–high heat for 3–5 minutes until lightly coloured. Add the minced meats, spices and ½ teaspoon salt and cook until browned, stirring occasionally. Stir in the garlic, sun-dried tomatoes and tomato purée and cook for 1 minute.

When the buckwheat is cooked, drain, add to the meat mixture and mix together well.

Preheat the oven to 200°C, 180°C fan (400°F), Gas Mark 6.

Butter 8 mini cocottes or other ovenproof dishes about 12cm (4½ inches) in diameter, or a 22cm (8½ inch) nonstick cake tin. Line with the cabbage leaves, overlapping and leaving some overhanging the sides and filling any gaps in the middle as necessary. Add the meat and buckwheat mixture to fill almost to the top and pat down. Cover with the remaining cabbage leaves to fully enclose the stuffing. Cover the pans or dishes with their lids if they have them or use foil. Bake for 20 minutes. Remove the lids or foil and bake for another 5–10 minutes if necessary to brown around the edges.

Remove from the oven and leave to rest for 10 minutes before turning out. Serve topped with crème fraîche and a dusting of paprika, garnished with dill sprigs.

PORK BELLY CASSEROLE

This hearty casserole combines tender pork belly with vegetables in a rich, smoky tomato sauce. Perfect served with mash, baked potatoes, grains or a crusty baguette. Add a dash of hot sauce if you like heat.

SERVES 4–6

1 tablespoon vegetable oil
350g (12oz) pork belly, rind removed, cut into 2cm (¾ inch) chunks
1½ tablespoons smoked paprika
1 onion, chopped
2 carrots, peeled and sliced into rounds
1 small parsnip, peeled and roughly chopped
3 garlic cloves, finely sliced
4 bay leaves
4 allspice berries
3 tablespoons tomato purée
200ml (7fl oz) vegetable stock
200ml (7fl oz) passata
200g (7oz) cherry tomatoes
400g (14oz) can baked beans
smoked salt and freshly ground black pepper

Heat a heavy-based pan over a medium–high heat and add the oil. Sear the pork belly for about 5 minutes until browned all over. Reduce the heat to low, sprinkle over the smoked paprika and toss to coat, then remove the meat and set aside.

Add the onion to the pan and cook for 3–5 minutes over a low heat until soft, stirring occasionally. Add the carrots, parsnip, garlic, bay leaves and allspice berries, stirring to combine. Return the pork to the pan and stir through the tomato purée, coating everything well. Cover the pan with a lid and simmer for 5 minutes.

Stir in the stock, passata and cherry tomatoes, re-cover and simmer gently for 30 minutes, stirring occasionally. Taste and adjust the seasoning with smoked salt and pepper.

Add the baked beans, cover again and simmer for 10–15 minutes until heated through, stirring occasionally. Season to taste again before serving hot.

STAUB
STAUB

WOJTEK'S BEANS
FASOLKA PO BRETOŃSKU

Growing up in Central Europe, this bean dish was often on our table – not quite a goulash, not quite a stew, but something even better than regular baked beans. I now add a hint of sweetness and smoky heat, which makes these beans irresistibly addictive. My family served them simply, with crusty bread or baby potatoes. This is one of those dishes that improves in flavour if left to the next day to serve, so make it ahead if you can.

SERVES 4–6

150g (5½oz) chorizo, chopped
100g (3½oz) smoked bacon lardons
150g (5½oz) Polish smoked sausage (*kielbasa*), sliced
1 onion, finely chopped
2 tablespoons tomato purée
2 garlic cloves, very finely chopped
6 allspice berries
3 tablespoons dried marjoram
1 tablespoon smoked paprika
1 tablespoon chipotle paste
500ml (18fl oz) passata
2 teaspoons sugar
4 bay leaves
2 x 400g (14oz) cans butter beans, drained
50g (1¾oz) sun-dried tomatoes in oil, drained and chopped
1 teaspoon smoked salt
salt and freshly ground black pepper
chopped chives, to garnish
soured cream or Greek yogurt, to serve

Heat a heavy-based pan over a medium heat, add the chorizo, bacon and sausage and cook, stirring occasionally, for 5–7 minutes until golden. Add the onion and cook for about 3 minutes until translucent.

Stir in the tomato purée, garlic, allspice berries, marjoram, smoked paprika and chipotle paste. Cook, stirring, for 1 minute, then stir in the passata, sugar and bay leaves and bring to a simmer.

Add the beans, sun-dried tomatoes and smoked salt. Cover the pan with a lid and simmer gently for 15 minutes. Taste and adjust the seasoning with salt and pepper, then re-cover and simmer for another 15 minutes.

Serve in bowls, garnished with a sprinkling of chopped chives, with soured cream or Greek yogurt on the side.

PIEROGI 3 WAYS

Nothing says Poland more than pierogi. Beloved comfort food, humble and a great equalizer of people around a table, I can barely write the word 'pierogi' without salivating. I owe my pierogi skills to my grandmother who taught me how to obtain a lovely dough that is as easy to work as it is to eat, and the ability to create mouthwatering fillings. The best way to proceed is to make the filling first, then prepare the dough (see recipe on page 107), assemble and cook. This is a staple of the Polish Christmas table, but any day is a good day to eat pierogi.

MAKES ENOUGH FOR ABOUT 80 PIEROGI

FOR THE POTATO FILLING

500g (1lb 2oz) all-rounder potatoes, peeled and cut into evenly sized chunks
50g (1¾oz) unsalted butter
2 small onions, finely chopped
100g (3½oz) smoked bacon lardons
250g (9oz) cottage cheese
salt and freshly ground black pepper
flat leaf parsley sprigs, to garnish

Cook the potatoes in a saucepan of lightly salted boiling water for 15–20 minutes until tender. Drain and mash, then set aside in the pan.

While the potatoes are cooking, melt the butter in a frying pan, add the onions and cook gently for about 7 minutes, or until golden. Transfer to a small plate. Add the lardons to the pan and fry over a medium–high heat for 3–5 minutes, or until browned. Transfer to a chopping board and chop finely.

Combine the onions and lardons, reserve one-third for garnishing and stir the rest into the mashed potatoes along with the cottage cheese. Taste and adjust the seasoning with salt and pepper. Leave the mixture to cool completely.

To prepare, fill and cook the pierogi, follow the instructions on page 107. Serve the pierogi garnished with the remaining fried onion-lardon mixture and flat leaf parsley sprigs.

MAKES ENOUGH FOR ABOUT 60 PIEROGI

FOR THE BEEF FILLING

500g (1lb 2oz) leftover cooked beef from a roast or stew, or raw beef brisket
2 carrots, peeled and chopped (if cooking brisket)
2 onions, roughly chopped (if cooking brisket)
1 bay leaf (if cooking brisket)
3–4 tablespoons vegetable oil
2 onions, finely chopped
soy or Worcestershire sauce, to taste (optional)
salt and freshly ground black pepper
1 small bunch of flat leaf parsley, finely chopped, to garnish

If using leftover cooked beef, mince finely in a food processor, then proceed to cooking the onions, below.

If using raw brisket, put into a saucepan and add cold water to almost cover. Season well with salt and add the carrots, the roughly chopped onions and the bay leaf.

Bring to the boil, then reduce the heat, cover the pan with a lid and simmer for about 2 hours, or until the meat is very tender. Top up the liquid if necessary to keep the meat at least part submerged.

Remove the meat and vegetables from the broth and leave to cool, then mince finely in a food processor, using some of the cooking liquid as necessary to make a soft mixture. Transfer to a bowl and set aside.

Heat the oil in a frying pan, add the finely chopped onion and cook gently for about 8 minutes until golden. Reserve one-third of the onion for garnishing and stir the rest into the meat. Taste and adjust the seasoning with salt and pepper, adding soy or Worcestershire sauce if desired. Leave the mixture to cool completely.

To prepare, fill and cook the pierogi, follow the instructions on page 107. Serve the pierogi garnished with the remaining fried onion and chopped parsley.

MAKES ENOUGH FOR ABOUT 70 PIEROGI

FOR THE SAUERKRAUT PORCINI FILLING

60g (2¼oz) dried porcini mushrooms
1 litre (1¾ pints) boiling water
3–4 tablespoons vegetable oil
2 onions, finely chopped
700g (1lb 9oz) sauerkraut, rinsed, drained and finely chopped
2 bay leaves
½ teaspoon ground allspice
½ teaspoon salt
½ teaspoon freshly ground black pepper

Put the dried mushrooms into a heatproof bowl, pour over the measured boiling water and leave to soak for at least 30 minutes.

Meanwhile, heat the oil in a frying pan, add the onions and cook gently for about 8 minutes until golden.

Strain the mushrooms, reserving the soaking liquid, and chop finely, then put into a large saucepan. Add the sauerkraut and onions, along with the reserved mushroom soaking liquid, bay leaves, allspice, salt and pepper. Mix together well.

Cover the pan with a lid and simmer over a low heat, stirring occasionally, for about 30 minutes until golden and caramelized and all the liquid has evaporated. Taste and if the mixture is too sour, stir in more water and continue simmering to soften the flavour. Repeat as needed. Remove the bay leaves and leave the mixture to cool completely.

To prepare, fill and cook the pierogi, follow the instructions on page 107.

MAKES 60–80 PIEROGI

FOR THE PIEROGI

500g (1lb 2oz) plain flour, plus extra for dusting
250ml (9fl oz) hot water
4 tablespoons vegetable oil
¼ teaspoon salt

NOTE: A full recipe of dough with one of the fillings will make 60–80 pierogi. For a smaller batch, halve the dough and filling recipes.

Sift the flour into a large mixing bowl. Add the measured hot water, oil and salt. Mix with a wooden spatula until the dough is cool enough to handle.

Transfer to a lightly floured work surface. Knead the dough vigorously for at least 10 minutes. Cover with a damp tea towel and leave to rest for 15 minutes.

Divide the dough into quarters. Working with one quarter at a time and keeping the unrolled pieces covered by the damp tea towel, roll out the dough evenly until thin enough so that you can just about see your hands through it.

Using a downturned glass with a rim 7–9cm (2¾–3½ inches) in diameter, cut out as many circles as you can from the dough, rerolling the scraps to cut out more.

Place a small spoonful of filling in each circle and fold the dough over in half to enclose the filling. Don't overfill or they may burst when cooking. Press the edges together to seal well. For a decorative edge, work around it pinching and then folding bit by bit. Alternatively, press around the edge with the tines of a fork to create a pattern, or just leave it plain.

As they are completed, place each filled and well-sealed pierogi on a lightly floured tray ready to cook. Line a separate large tray with kitchen paper.

Bring a large saucepan of salted water to the boil, then reduce to a gentle simmer. Add the pierogi, in batches of 5 or 6, and cook for 3–5 minutes until they bob up to the surface. Remove with a slotted spoon and leave to drain on the lined tray while you finish cooking the remaining pierogi.

PASTA WITH CLAMS & GIN

At Wojtek's Bistro, I've broken with a few traditions, first by serving my take on vongole with paccheri instead of the usual spaghetti. Guests are always surprised by how much better it works – those wide tubes carry the briny juices perfectly, so no chasing clams around the plate. And I replace wine with gin for the cooking, which makes it so special. What I love most is how impressive this dish looks while being genuinely effortless. Pair it with crisp white wine or even a G&T at the table, and don't forget to offer plenty of baguette for mopping up those incredible juices.

SERVES 4

1kg (2lb 4oz) clams
500g (1lb 2oz) large dried pasta shapes, such as paccheri
1–2 tablespoons extra virgin olive oil
450g (1lb) cherry tomatoes, halved
3 garlic cloves, finely sliced
5 tablespoons gin, preferably Tanqueray
1 large bunch of flat leaf parsley, chopped
fine salt and freshly ground black pepper

Rinse the clams in cold running water and scrub the shells if necessary. Put into a large bowl, cover with cold water and salt generously. Leave to soak for 2–3 hours, then drain and rinse well to remove any grit. Discard any with damaged shells.

Bring a large saucepan of salted water to the boil. Add the pasta to the boiling water and cook according to the packet instructions, then drain.

Meanwhile, heat the olive oil in a heavy-based pan, add the tomatoes and garlic and season lightly with salt and pepper. Cover the pan with a lid and cook over a medium heat for 5–10 minutes until soft. Add the gin and cook, uncovered, for 2 minutes.

Add the clams and half the parsley, then increase the heat, re-cover the pan and cook for about 5 minutes until all the clams have opened.

Turn off the heat and stir in the pasta, then serve in bowls, scattered with the remaining chopped parsley.

PAPRIKA PRAWNS & BUCKWHEAT

Mine is a family of buckwheat eaters and I still find I have a preference for grains over root vegetables when considering what to cook and eat. Here, this nutty grain goes so well with the spicy richness of the paprika-red prawns, while the smoked salt adds a contemporary twist.

SERVES 2–4

8 large raw shell-on prawns
1 tablespoon sweet paprika
1 tablespoon smoked paprika
1 tablespoon smoked salt
1 teaspoon coarsely ground black pepper
60g (2¼oz) butter
2 garlic cloves, thinly sliced
chopped flat leaf parsley, to garnish

FOR THE BUCKWHEAT
2 tablespoons extra virgin olive oil
1 onion, halved and sliced
100g (3½oz) toasted buckwheat (*kasha*), cooked (see page 93)
smoked salt and freshly ground black pepper

To keep the prawns from bending as they cook, on the underside, insert a cocktail stick lengthways through each prawn from head to tail. Set aside. If you don't mind curly prawns, cook as is.

Mix together the sweet and smoked paprika, smoked salt and pepper in a small bowl. Sprinkle the spice mixture evenly over the prawns on both sides. Cover and set aside.

For the buckwheat, heat the oil in a frying pan, add the onion and cook for 3–5 minutes until translucent. Season to taste with smoked salt and pepper and set aside.

To cook the prawns, heat the butter in a separate frying pan large enough to hold them in a single layer. When foaming, add the prawns and garlic and cook over a medium heat for 2–3 minutes, then turn and cook the other side for 2–3 minutes, or until pink throughout. Remove the pan from the heat and set aside.

Add the cooked buckwheat to the onion and reheat, stirring until hot throughout.

To serve, transfer the buckwheat to a serving dish and arrange the prawns on top, drizzling over the pan juices. Sprinkle with chopped flat leaf parsley to garnish.

WHITE FISH & TOMATO BAKE
RYBA PO GRECKU

The Polish name for this dish translates as 'Greek-style fish', but it has nothing to do with Greece and no one can convincingly explain why it is called that. It's a traditional part of the Polish Christmas table, but my family often made it all throughout the colder months. I always preferred mine warm, while the other family members preferred it cold with thick slices of sourdough bread. Whatever temperature suits you best, this is decidedly better the day after it is made.

SERVES 4–6

about 175ml (6fl oz) vegetable oil
2 large carrots, peeled and grated
1 large parsnip, peeled and grated
350g (12oz) celeriac, peeled and grated
1 large onion, finely chopped
1 leek, trimmed, halved, cleaned and thinly sliced
4 bay leaves
6 allspice berries
50ml (2fl oz) water
5 tablespoons tomato purée
400g (14oz) can chopped tomatoes
1 teaspoon paprika
4–5 tablespoons plain flour
700g (1lb 9oz) skinless fish fillets, such as haddock
fine salt and freshly ground black pepper
curly parsley sprigs, to garnish

Heat 4–5 tablespoons of the oil in a large saucepan, add the carrots, parsnip, celeriac, onion and leek and cook, stirring, for 8–10 minutes until softened, adding more oil as needed. Season well with salt and pepper, then add the bay leaves, allspice berries and measured water and mix together well. Cover the pan with a lid and simmer gently for 20 minutes, stirring once or twice.

Stir in the tomato purée, canned tomatoes and paprika. Taste and adjust the seasoning, then re-cover and continue to simmer while you prepare the fish.

Preheat the oven to 200°C, 180°C fan (400°F), Gas Mark 6.

Put the flour on a plate and mix with 1 teaspoon salt. Heat 4–5 tablespoons of the oil in a large frying pan over a medium heat. Once hot, dredge the fish in the seasoned flour to coat on both sides, then add to the oil; you may need to work in batches. Cook for 3–5 minutes on each side until browned. Set aside on a plate and season lightly with salt.

Spread one-third of the vegetable mixture in an even layer to cover the base of a large shallow ovenproof dish with a lid. Arrange the fish fillets on top and spread the remaining vegetable mixture over to completely cover the fish. Cover with the lid and bake for 30 minutes. Serve hot, warm or cold, garnished with curly parsley sprigs.

CHAPTER 4

KITCHEN-GARDEN COOKING

PASTA WITH CHANTERELLES & MISO

There are some strong flavours going on in this dish: earthy mushrooms meet lashings of cream and butter, plus miso and Comté. I prefer to match these potent elements with an alcoholic beverage of the same rank, so I don't use an ordinary wine here. Sherry is traditional with mushrooms but I have been known to make this with homemade quince liqueur (see page 200). Simple but effective.

SERVES 2

40g (1½oz) unsalted butter
1 small onion, finely chopped
1 garlic clove, sliced
300g (10½oz) chanterelle mushrooms, cleaned (see Note, page 59) and roughly chopped
1 tablespoon white miso
50ml (2fl oz) dry sherry
200g (7oz) dried pasta shapes
50ml (2fl oz) crème fraîche or soured cream
salt and freshly ground black pepper
chopped flat leaf parsley, to garnish
Comté cheese, to serve

Melt half the butter in a large shallow flameproof casserole dish with a lid. Add the onion and garlic and cook over a medium heat for 2–3 minutes. Stir in the mushrooms and the remaining butter, cover the pan with the lid and cook for 10 minutes, stirring occasionally.

Blend the miso with the sherry in a small bowl. Stir the miso mixture into the mushrooms, re-cover and simmer gently for 5 minutes.

Meanwhile, bring a large saucepan of salted water to the boil. Add the pasta and cook according to the packet instructions.

When the pasta is almost ready, stir the crème fraîche or soured cream into the mushroom mixture. Taste and adjust the seasoning with salt and pepper. Drain the pasta and add it to the mushroom mixture, then toss together gently.

Divide the pasta and sauce between 2 bowls, grate over the Comté and sprinkle with chopped flat leaf parsley to garnish. Serve immediately.

CHERRY TOMATO & BUTTER PASTA

Sweet, saucy and wonderfully speedy, I use cherry tomatoes in this dish since they're so much more flavourful than the bigger ones, and cooking transforms them into a gorgeous tomato confit that I can't get enough of. My grandmother always used butter for her tomato pasta sauces because, along with sunflower oil, it was traditionally the main cooking fat in Poland. She would sometimes top this with goats' cheese, but I'm a Comté person myself. This works very well as a quick supper for two – simply halve the recipe.

SERVES 4

100g (3½oz) unsalted butter
1 onion, quartered
1kg (2lb 4oz) cherry tomatoes
400g (14oz) dried pasta, such as paccheri
salt and freshly ground black pepper
grated Comté cheese or other hard cheese, to serve

Put the butter and onion in a large heavy-based pan over a low heat. Cover the pan with a lid and heat for about 3 minutes until the butter is melted and sizzling.

Meanwhile, fill a large saucepan with well-salted water and bring to the boil.

Add the tomatoes to the butter and onion and season lightly with salt and pepper. Re-cover and cook over a low heat for 15 minutes.

While the tomatoes are cooking, add the pasta to the boiling water and cook according to the packet instructions.

When the tomatoes are cooked, use a stick blender to blend the sauce; it should be smooth but still rustic.

Using tongs, transfer the pasta to the sauce along with some of the cooking water and cook gently for a few minutes, stirring to coat the pasta with the sauce. Taste and adjust the seasoning, then serve topped with grated cheese.

STAUB

STAUB

SUMMER STEW
LECZO

Every summer, when peppers and tomatoes are abundant in Poland, this dish appears on tables across the country. My version honours tradition but adds a few personal touches: for instance, I peel my tomatoes for silkiness, though canned work beautifully for busy days. The magic happens when vegetables slowly soften with smoked sausage, building deep, rich flavour. While this is delicious straight away, it tastes even better the next day. Serve it with crusty bread for a light meal, or top it with fried eggs for the perfect brunch.

SERVES 2–4

500g (1lb 2oz) peppers (preferably red but any colour works), cored and deseeded
600g (1lb 5oz) ripe tomatoes, peeled, if you like
2 onions, peeled
650g (1lb 7oz) courgettes
about 200g (7oz) Polish smoked sausage (*kielbasa*) or smoked bacon lardons
extra virgin olive oil or vegetable oil, for cooking
4 garlic cloves, very finely chopped
2 teaspoons paprika
1 teaspoon Tabasco sauce (optional)
salt and freshly ground black pepper
bread, to serve

All the vegetable pieces need to be about the same size, so begin by cutting the peppers into chunks, then proceed with the tomatoes, onions and courgettes.

Chop the smoked sausage, if using, into the same-sized chunks as the vegetables.

Heat a generous glug of oil in a sauté pan with a lid. When hot but not smoking, add the sausage or lardons and onion and cook over a medium heat for 3–5 minutes, or until golden brown. Stir in the garlic and cook for 1 minute.

Stir in the peppers, cover the pan with the lid and cook over a low heat for 15 minutes, stirring occasionally as they soften.

Add the courgettes, tomatoes and paprika, season to taste with salt and pepper and stir well. Re-cover and continue cooking over a low heat for 15 minutes. Taste and adjust the seasoning, adding the Tabasco if desired.

Serve hot or at room temperature with bread to mop up the juices.

ROASTED CABBAGE WEDGES

Growing up in Poland, I ate cabbage in countless ways. I always had a particular fondness for the way Grandma would bake it with her homemade summer tomato purée, creating the most incredible flavours. This recipe honours that tradition, but with a modern twist I discovered at a British restaurant years ago: searing and roasting the cabbage transforms this humble vegetable into something genuinely exciting.

SERVES 2

60g (2¼oz) unsalted butter
1 Savoy cabbage, about 500g (1lb 2oz), outer leaves removed, quartered
500ml (18fl oz) vegetable stock
4 tablespoons tomato purée
1 bay leaf
¼ teaspoon ground allspice
1 teaspoon sugar
salt and coarsely ground black pepper
chopped fresh herbs, such as thyme, marjoram and parsley, to garnish

Preheat the oven to 180°C, 160°C fan (350°F), Gas Mark 4.

Melt the butter in a frying pan, add the cabbage wedges and cook over a medium–high heat for 3–5 minutes on each cut side until caramelized. Remove to a plate and season with salt and pepper.

Add the remaining ingredients to the pan and cook, stirring, until well blended. Taste and adjust the seasoning.

Transfer the cabbage wedges to an ovenproof dish just large enough to hold them and pour over the sauce. Roast for 20 minutes, then turn so that the other side faces up, baste and continue roasting for another 15–20 minutes until nicely browned. Serve immediately, scattered with chopped fresh herbs to garnish.

STAUB

CABBAGE ROLLS
GOŁĄBKI

An East meets West take on this Polish classic. I once had a Korean flatmate who got me accustomed to gochujang in everything, and I think this secret ingredient makes a stupendous contribution to what is already a stellar recipe – Grandma's, of course. Pickle lovers should serve this with Polish pickled cucumbers alongside (see page 205 for homemade).

SERVES 6–8

1 tablespoon vegetable oil
1 onion, finely chopped
1 Savoy or white cabbage
750g (1lb 10oz) mixed minced pork and beef
200g (7oz) toasted buckwheat (*kasha*), cooked (see page 93) and cooled
1½ tablespoons salt
1 teaspoon ground nutmeg
2 tablespoons gochujang
4 bay leaves
6 allspice berries
500ml (18fl oz) vegetable stock
dill sprigs, to garnish

FOR THE TOMATO SAUCE
500ml (18fl oz) passata
¼ teaspoon ground nutmeg
¼ teaspoon ground allspice
½ teaspoon salt

Heat the oil in a frying pan, add the onion and cook over a medium heat for about 3 minutes until translucent. Set aside.

Bring a large saucepan of water to the boil. Cut out as much of the cabbage core as possible and carefully peel away the outer leaves, keeping them intact. Working in batches, blanch the cabbage leaves in the boiling water for 3–5 minutes. Remove carefully and place on kitchen paper to drain and cool. Depending on size, you will need about 12–14 big leaves, but blanch more for patching and lining the base of your ovenproof dish.

Meanwhile, make the filling. Put the minced meat, cooked buckwheat, salt, nutmeg and gochujang into a large bowl and mix together well.

Line a large ovenproof dish, preferably with a lid (or use foil to cover), with some of the less perfect blanched cabbage leaves.

Preheat the oven to 200°C, 180°C fan (400°F), Gas Mark 6.

Working with one cabbage leaf at a time, lay it on the work surface and trim away any thick core that may interfere with rolling. Place a spoonful of the meat mixture in the middle. Fold over one side to part enclose, then the other, and roll up, tucking in the ends to enclose the filling. Arrange, folded-side down, in the dish. Repeat until all the leaves are filled; the rolls can be packed tightly in the dish. Arrange the bay leaves and allspice berries on top and pour over the stock to come up just less than halfway. Cover with the lid or foil and bake for 30 minutes.

Meanwhile, put all the sauce ingredients into a saucepan and heat until warmed through, stirring occasionally.

Remove the dish from the oven, then pour over the sauce and spread evenly, pushing down lightly with the back of a spoon to blend the cooking juices with the sauce. Re-cover with the lid or foil and bake for another 20 minutes. Uncover and bake for a final 15–20 minutes until nicely browned on top. Garnish with dill sprigs and serve hot.

BRAISED CABBAGE WITH SMOKED SAUSAGE

This hearty one-pot meal brings together the smoky richness of Polish smoked sausage (*kielbasa*), sweet carrots and tender cabbage, all infused with caraway seeds and a touch of paprika. Ready in no time, it's the perfect weeknight meal that captures the essence of Polish home cooking: simple ingredients transformed into pure comfort food. Serve with lots of crusty bread or mash, or both.

SERVES 4–6

50g (1¾oz) unsalted butter, or more if needed
1 onion, halved and sliced
200g (7oz) Polish smoked sausage (*kielbasa*), chopped
2 large carrots, peeled and sliced
1 teaspoon caraway seeds
½ teaspoon paprika
500g (1lb 2oz) Hispi or white cabbage, cored and roughly chopped
250ml (9fl oz) water
200g (7oz) can chopped tomatoes or 1 large ripe fresh tomato, chopped
2 teaspoons fine salt, or more to taste
1 teaspoon sugar
lemon juice, to taste
freshly ground black pepper
dill sprigs, to garnish
soured cream, to serve

Melt the butter in a large shallow pan with a lid, add the onion and sausage and cook over a medium heat for 3–5 minutes until the onion is translucent. Add the carrots, caraway seeds and paprika and cook for about 5 minutes, stirring occasionally.

Add more butter, if necessary, and stir in the cabbage. Cook for 3–5 minutes until softened, stirring occasionally.

Add the measured water, tomatoes, salt and sugar. Mix well, then reduce the heat, cover the pan with the lid and simmer gently for 20 minutes, stirring halfway through. Taste and adjust the seasoning with salt and pepper, then re-cover and continue simmering for another 20 minutes.

Add lemon juice as desired and serve topped with soured cream and a grinding of pepper, garnished with dill sprigs.

STAUB
STAUB
STAUB
STAUB
STAUB
STAUB

SAUERKRAUT & MUSHROOMS WITH DIAMOND NOODLES ŁAZANKI

In southern Poland, diamond-shaped noodles reign supreme. This is where my father's family is from, and it was there, during childhood visits to paternal relations, that I connected with this dish. In a sprawling country kitchen, all 13 cousins would scramble into position, eager to have enough room on the counter to cut our own perfect little dough diamonds. Cooking this brings all that joy back to my London kitchen.

SERVES 4

- 2 tablespoons vegetable oil, or more if needed
- 1 onion, chopped
- 200g (7oz) chestnut mushrooms, chopped
- 350g (12oz) sauerkraut, drained and chopped
- 4 allspice berries
- 1 teaspoon ground turmeric
- 1 teaspoon sugar
- 100ml (3½fl oz) vegetable stock
- salt and freshly ground black pepper
- chopped flat leaf parsley, to garnish

FOR THE NOODLES

- 125g (4½oz) plain flour, plus extra for dusting
- 1 egg plus 1 egg yolk, beaten together
- 25ml (1fl oz) water
- 1 teaspoon vegetable oil

For the noodles, mound the flour on a clean work surface and make a well in the middle. Add the eggs, then gradually work in the flour. Add the measured water and the oil and continue mixing until you can form the rough dough into a ball. Dust lightly with flour, if sticky, and knead vigorously for 3–5 minutes until smooth. Shape into a ball, cover with an upturned bowl and leave to rest for 15–20 minutes.

Meanwhile, heat the oil in a large frying pan with a lid, add the onion and cook over a medium heat for 3–5 minutes until translucent. Increase the heat, add the mushrooms, along with more oil if needed, and cook for 5 minutes until just golden. Stir in the sauerkraut with the remaining ingredients and mix well, then cover the pan with the lid and simmer gently for 20 minutes, stirring occasionally.

Once the noodles have finished resting, bring a saucepan of salted water to the boil.

Roll the dough out on a lightly floured work surface as thinly as you can without tearing. Cut the sheet into strips 2cm (¾ inch) wide, then cut the strips into diamond shapes. Add to the boiling water and cook for about 3 minutes until the noodles rise to the surface.

Drain and add to the sauerkraut mixture, stirring gently to mix well. Taste and adjust the seasoning with salt and pepper. Serve hot, sprinkled with chopped flat leaf parsley.

POTATO DAUPHINOISE À LA WOJTEK

This luxurious gratin uses miso and smoked salt to add savoury depth, while allspice and bay keep it firmly anchored in Polish tradition. The result is a dish that is both comforting and sophisticated, perfect as a side for roasts or as a vegetarian main course.

SERVES 4

400ml (14fl oz) whole milk
400ml (14fl oz) double cream
3 garlic cloves, crushed
4 bay leaves, preferably fresh
4–6 allspice berries or ¼ teaspoon ground allspice
1kg (2lb 4oz) potatoes (any all-rounder variety)
2–3 teaspoons smoked salt
1 teaspoon freshly ground black pepper
30g (1oz) white miso
30–50g (1–1¾oz) Comté cheese or other hard cheese, grated

Pour the milk and cream into a saucepan, add the garlic, bay leaves and allspice and bring to a simmer. Remove from the heat, cover the pan with a lid and leave to infuse for 10–20 minutes.

Meanwhile, preheat the oven to 180°C, 160°C fan (350°F), Gas Mark 4.

Peel the potatoes, then use a mandoline to thinly slice. Arrange the slices, overlapping, in a 26cm (10½ inch) ovenproof frying pan or a 30 x 18cm (12 x 7 inch) ovenproof dish, seasoning with the smoked salt and pepper as you go.

Add the miso to the infused cream mixture and stir well to dissolve. Pour over the potatoes, ensuring the bay leaves, allspice and garlic are evenly distributed, and bake for 30 minutes.

Remove from the oven and scatter over the grated cheese evenly. Return to the oven and continue baking for another 15–20 minutes until golden and gorgeously fragrant. Serve hot.

STAUB

CAESAR SALAD WITH FRESH SWEETCORN

For me, there's nothing more fantastic in the salad department than a Caesar. It's easy, crunchy and deliciously filling – the kind of dish that never gets old. Growing up in 1980s Poland, my mum used to make her own version with sweetcorn and just mayo, since not many people knew about the traditional recipe back then, but I loved it all the same. Over the years, I've been developing my own take on this classic, tweaking and perfecting it until it's become something I genuinely crave, and I think you will, too.

SERVES 4–6

5 Little Gem lettuces
2 cooked chicken breasts, meat shredded
1 cooked sweetcorn cob, kernels stripped
100g (3½oz) croutons
hard cheese, such as Comté or Parmesan, to serve

FOR THE DRESSING
2 egg yolks
4 tablespoons best-quality mayonnaise (see page 204 for homemade)
juice of 1 lime, plus extra to taste
2–3 anchovy fillets, mashed
1 teaspoon Worcestershire sauce
salt and freshly ground black pepper

First, make the dressing. Put all the ingredients into a bowl and mix together. Taste and adjust the seasoning, adding more lime juice as desired. Cover and refrigerate until needed.

Separate the lettuce leaves and arrange on a serving platter. Top with the shredded chicken and sweetcorn kernels, and scatter over the croutons.

Finely grate over a layer of cheese, then spoon over the dressing. Serve immediately.

QUINOA SALAD WITH ASPARAGUS, PEA & FETA

Quinoa sounded so exotic growing up, yet my avant-garde grandmother used it all the time. For some reason, we kids were particularly drawn to it, probably because the neutral taste made it the perfect blank canvas for whatever seasonings she would add. That's actually quinoa's greatest strength: it's incredibly versatile and soaks up whatever flavours you team it with.

SERVES 2

200g (7oz) quinoa
20g (¾oz) butter
80g (3oz) frozen peas
120g (4¼oz) asparagus, cut into bite-sized pieces
50g (1¾oz) feta cheese, crumbled
mint leaves, to garnish

FOR THE DRESSING
juice of ½ lemon
1 teaspoon clear honey
3 tablespoons extra virgin olive oil
fine sea salt and freshly ground black pepper

Cook the quinoa according to the packet instructions, then leave to cool.

Meanwhile, melt the butter in a saucepan, add the peas and asparagus and pour in enough water to cover. Cover the pan with a lid and simmer gently for 5–7 minutes until the vegetables are tender. Drain and leave to cool.

Whisk the dressing ingredients together.

Put the quinoa, peas and asparagus into a mixing bowl. Add the dressing and feta and toss together. Taste and adjust the seasoning as desired.

Transfer to a serving plate and garnish with mint leaves before serving.

POTATO & VEGETABLE SALAD OLIVIER
SAŁATKA JARZYNOWA

Polish cooking can be defined by its resourcefulness. The traditional way to prepare this classic is a perfect example: put everything in one pan and cook together to conserve water, energy and time. And it works. Besides its practicality, there is so much to love about this recipe. It's retro and modern at the same time, and so easy to adapt. Some people add tuna or sweetcorn, or cubes of cooked ham or smoked fish. My grandmother preferred sun-dried tomatoes for an extra hit of umami and colour. This salad improves over time.

SERVES 6–8

500g (1lb 2oz) potatoes, peeled
2 carrots (about 200g/7oz), peeled
1 parsnip (about 250g/9oz), peeled
150–180g (5½–6¼oz) celeriac, peeled
2 eggs
½ apple, cored
3 medium Polish pickled cucumbers in vinegar (*konserwowe*; see page 205 for homemade)
300g (10½oz) can peas, drained
50g (1¾oz) sun-dried tomatoes in oil, drained and patted dry
4 heaped tablespoons good-quality mayonnaise (see page 204 for homemade)
1 teaspoon Dijon or Polish mustard
1 small bunch of flat leaf parsley, finely chopped, plus extra sprigs to garnish
salt and freshly ground black pepper
crusty baguette, to serve

Fill a large saucepan with cold water. Add salt and then the potatoes, carrots, parsnip, celeriac and the eggs in their shells. Bring to the boil, then reduce the heat to a simmer.

Remove the eggs after 8 minutes and continue cooking for 15–20 minutes until all the vegetables are tender. Check them regularly for doneness by piercing with a fork, as they may not all cook at exactly the same pace, depending on size, and you may need to remove some while others finish cooking. When all are cooked, drain and leave to cool.

Meanwhile, chop the apple and pickled cucumbers into pieces about the size of a pea. Put into a large mixing bowl with the peas.

Chop all the cooked vegetables (reserving a little of the carrot, sliced, for garnishing, if desired) and the sun-dried tomatoes into pea-sized pieces and add to the bowl.

Shell the eggs and also chop into pea-sized pieces, then add to the bowl.

Add the mayonnaise, mustard, parsley and salt and pepper to taste and mix together well. The salad will not taste well-seasoned at this stage. However, once covered and refrigerated for a few hours, the flavours will have developed, so taste again and adjust the seasoning before serving. Garnish with the reserved carrot slices, if desired, and parsley sprigs, and serve with crusty baguette.

CUCUMBER SALAD
MIZERIA

Every Polish household knows that when summer arrives with its sweltering days and gardens overflowing with cucumbers, it's time for *mizeria*. I hated picking cucumbers as a kid, having to reach for them hidden under their scratchy leaves – definitely misery for me! But the moment this cool, creamy salad hit the lunch table alongside golden-brown meatballs and buttery potatoes, all showered with fresh dill, I quickly forgot my cucumber-picking complaints. This ridiculously simple dish is pure summer nostalgia, the taste of a Polish childhood in one bowl.

SERVES 4

500g (1lb 2oz) cucumber
1 heaped teaspoon salt, or more to taste
1 teaspoon rice vinegar
1 teaspoon sugar
4 tablespoons soured cream or Greek yogurt
a few dill sprigs
freshly ground black pepper

Using a mandoline, peel the cucumber, then carefully slice it thinly into a mixing bowl.

Add the salt, toss gently and leave to stand for 10 minutes to extract the excess liquid from the cucumber.

Working with a handful at a time, gently squeeze the cucumber slices over the sink to extract any remaining juices and transfer to a platter or salad bowl.

Add the vinegar and sugar and toss gently, then add the soured cream or yogurt, dill and pepper. Taste and adjust the seasoning.

Serve immediately, or cover and refrigerate and serve within a few hours.

CELERIAC, APPLE & RAISIN SLAW
SURÓWKA Z SELERA

This old-school Polish side dish was my grandmother's clever way of getting her grandchildren to eat vegetables. She was wise because without those raisins we probably wouldn't have touched it. Now, as an adult, I fully appreciate what she knew all along: the nutty flavour and texture of celeriac paired with sweet bites of raisin and crisp apple is absolutely wonderful, no bribing required.

SERVES 2–4

350g (12oz) celeriac, peeled and grated
1 apple, peeled, cored and grated
40g (1½oz) raisins or sultanas
2 tablespoons good-quality mayonnaise (see page 204 for homemade)
2 tablespoons Greek yogurt
juice of ½ lemon
fine salt and freshly ground black pepper
flat leaf parsley sprigs, to garnish

Put all the ingredients into a mixing bowl and mix together well. Taste and adjust the seasoning. This can be eaten straight away, but it is even tastier if covered and refrigerated overnight.

Serve garnished with flat leaf parsley sprigs.

LEEK, CARROT & APPLE REMOULADE
SURÓWKA Z PORA I MARCHWII

Both my grandmother and my mother knew I would only eat this if the leeks were cooked, so they would blanch the sliced leek first, though it's traditionally kept raw. As with most Polish slaws, this is brilliant alongside practically any dish, though I'll happily polish off a bowl on its own. As with most slaws, it's best to adjust the seasoning after the flavours have developed rather than immediately after it is made, as the vegetables need time to absorb the seasoning.

SERVES 4

300g (10½oz) trimmed leek, cleaned
1 carrot, peeled
1 apple, peeled and cored
2 tablespoons good-quality mayonnaise (see page 204 for homemade)
2 tablespoons crème fraîche or Greek yogurt
juice of 1 lemon
salt and freshly ground black pepper
dill sprigs, to garnish (optional)

Bring a saucepan of salted water to the boil.

Cut the leek in half lengthways, then cut each half in half widthways. Blanch the leek ribbons in the boiling water for 2–3 minutes, then drain thoroughly and leave to cool completely.

Meanwhile, using a box grater, grate the carrot and apple, then put them into a mixing bowl.

Whisk together the mayonnaise, crème fraîche or yogurt and half the lemon juice in a small bowl, seasoning with a pinch of salt and pepper. Set aside.

Add the cooled leek to the grated carrot and apple and toss gently together, then fold through the dressing until everything is well coated.

Cover and leave to stand for at least 30 minutes before serving. Taste and add more lemon juice if desired, then adjust the seasoning with salt before serving with a good grinding of pepper, garnished with dill sprigs if desired.

STAINLESS STEEL

SAUERKRAUT SALAD
SURÓWKA Z KISZONEJ KAPUSTY

One of the dangers of growing up in a Polish household is that this salad appears on the table with alarming regularity, more times than I can count, truly, and yet its appeal never lessens. There's something wonderful about this retro classic that still feels completely relevant. Maybe it's the punchy tang that cuts through rich dishes or the way it somehow complements absolutely everything. It's also endlessly adaptable. If you fancy a bit of heat, just toss in some finely chopped chilli, or if you prefer things milder, a quick rinse of the kraut and a little less sugar will do the trick. Once you've made this, you'll understand why Polish families have been serving it at lunch for generations.

SERVES 4–6

500g (1lb 2oz) sauerkraut
2 carrots, peeled and grated
1 large apple, peeled, cored and grated, plus unpeeled apple crescents to garnish
1 small onion, finely chopped
1 tablespoon caster sugar
1 teaspoon freshly ground black pepper
4 tablespoons vegetable oil
flat leaf parsley sprigs, to garnish

Drain the sauerkraut, reserving the brine.

Roughly chop the drained sauerkraut and put it into a mixing bowl.

Add the remaining ingredients and stir to blend thoroughly. Taste, and if the salad seems too dry, add 2–3 tablespoons of the reserved sauerkraut brine. Taste again and adjust the seasonings as desired.

Serve garnished with apple crescents and flat leaf parsley sprigs.

RED CABBAGE & APPLE SLAW
SURÓWKA Z CZERWONEJ KAPUSTY

This vibrant slaw is a staple of the Polish table, traditionally served alongside meat dishes; I especially like it with roast duck. The combination of sweet apples and tangy red cabbage creates the perfect balance, while the simple dressing brings everything together. It's incredibly moreish and very easy to eat just on its own, but you can also pile it onto sandwiches or enjoy it as part of a spread of varied Polish slaws. Best of all, it tastes even better after a day in the fridge.

SERVES 6–8

½ red cabbage, quartered and cored
1 apple, peeled and cored
1 large carrot, peeled
1 small red onion, halved
1 small bunch of flat leaf parsley, finely chopped
1 small bunch of dill, to garnish

FOR THE DRESSING
3 tablespoons cider vinegar or rice vinegar
3 tablespoons good-quality mayonnaise (see page 204 for homemade)
1 teaspoon fine salt
1 teaspoon freshly ground black pepper
1 teaspoon sugar

For the dressing, mix the ingredients together in a small bowl. Set aside.

Using a mandoline, carefully slice the cabbage thinly into a large mixing bowl.

Using a box grater, grate the apple, carrot and onion, then add to the cabbage along with the parsley.

Add the dressing and toss to combine thoroughly. Cover and leave to stand for at least 30 minutes before serving. This can also be made up to a day in advance and refrigerated until needed.

Serve garnished with the dill.

TOMATO, ONION & SOURED CREAM SALAD
POMIDORY ZE ŚMIETANĄ

There is so little to this dish and yet it is exceptional. Not all salads need to be dressed with an acidic sauce; in fact, cream on its own as a dressing was not uncommon once upon a time. It is a tradition that needs to be revived. Family legend has it that when my mother was pregnant, this was her main craving, with lots of bread to help mop up the succulent sauce.

SERVES 2

4–5 tablespoons soured cream or crème fraîche
500g (1lb 2oz) ripe tomatoes at room temperature, cut into wedges or chopped
1 small onion, halved and thinly sliced
a few dill sprigs, chopped
salt and freshly ground black pepper

Spread a plate with some of the soured cream or crème fraîche and top with some of the tomatoes. Dollop the remaining soured cream or crème fraîche in the middle and add the remaining tomatoes. Finish with the onion, dill, salt and lots of pepper.

Cover and leave to stand (only in the fridge if it's a hot day) for at least 30 minutes before serving.

WATERMELON & FETA SUMMER SALAD

When I think back to our garden giving an abundance of watermelon and Grandma making fresh Polish feta-style cheese from the neighbours' goats' and sheep's milk, there's only one dish to make to honour this memory. Toss in some crisp onions and crunchy croutons, and you've got the perfect light meal for summertime. Ridiculously easy, seriously delicious and best served ice cold.

SERVES 2–4

500g (1lb 2oz) peeled, deseeded watermelon, cut into small cubes
200g (7oz) feta cheese, cut into small cubes
100g (3½oz) croutons
½ red onion, thinly sliced
30g (1oz) shelled pistachio nuts, chopped
6 mint leaves, plus an extra sprig to garnish

FOR THE DRESSING
2 tablespoons sherry or cider vinegar
2 tablespoons extra virgin olive oil
salt and freshly ground black pepper

Whisk the dressing ingredients together.

Put the watermelon, feta, croutons and onion into a large bowl. Add the dressing and toss together gently.

Scatter over the pistachios and mint leaves, garnish with the mint sprig and serve immediately.

PEACH, TOMATO & FETA SUMMER SALAD

This refreshing salad is all about keeping things cool, literally. Prep it a few hours ahead, let everything chill in the fridge and only take it out just before serving. The cold ingredients make it especially delicious.

SERVES 4

500g (1lb 2oz) ripe tomatoes, cored
1 large ripe peach, about 200g (7oz), stoned
2–3 apricots, about 100g (3½oz) total weight, stoned
100g (3½oz) feta cheese, crumbled
30g (1oz) shelled pistachio nuts, chopped
mint leaves, to garnish

FOR THE DRESSING
2 tablespoons sherry or cider vinegar
2 tablespoons extra virgin olive oil
salt and freshly ground black pepper

Whisk the dressing ingredients together.

Slice the tomatoes, peach and apricots into crescents and arrange on a serving platter. Drizzle with the dressing, then scatter over the feta and pistachios. Garnish with mint leaves and serve.

NOTE: Feel free to swap the mint for basil, and if you've got pickled red onions on hand (see page 214 for homemade), they add just the right tang against the sweet peach.

CHAPTER 5

SWEET THINGS

APPLE PANCAKES
RACUCHY

These pancakes distinguish themselves by being thick, fluffy and studded with sweet-tart apple pieces, which add a beautiful texture to every bite. A staple of any Polish childhood, these are brilliant for breakfast or pudding, with a dusting of icing sugar. Simple, comforting and absolutely delicious.

MAKES 10–12 PANCAKES

2 eggs
30g (1oz) caster sugar
250g (9oz) plain flour
½ teaspoon bicarbonate of soda
½ teaspoon baking powder
pinch of salt
250ml (9fl oz) whole milk
2 apples, peeled, cored and grated
unsalted or clarified butter, for cooking
icing sugar, for dusting
homemade jam, to serve (optional)

Using a hand-held electric mixer on high speed, whisk the eggs and sugar together in a large mixing bowl for 3–5 minutes until frothy and almost doubled in volume.

Sift over the dry ingredients, add the milk and stir well until almost smooth. Stir in the apple.

Heat a large frying pan lightly greased with butter. Add the batter in large spoonfuls, about 3 or 4 at a time, and cook over a medium heat until you see bubbles on the surface and the edges are browning. Check for good browning on the undersides, then turn the pancakes over and cook on the other side until golden brown.

Keep the cooked pancakes covered with a clean tea towel while you cook the rest of the batter.

Serve warm with a dusting of icing sugar and a little homemade jam, if you like.

POLISH APPLE PIE
SZARLOTKA

You can't get more Polish than this apple pie, and most Polish children learn to bake by making it as their very first bake. It was mine, too, though my actual first culinary experiment was mixing cement and egg yolks at my grandfather's garage! The key to achieving the best result is using the right apples. You want tart varieties for acidity and firm ones that hold their shape when baked, so mixing two or three types is the solution.

SERVES 6–8

200g (7oz) cold unsalted butter, cut into small cubes, plus extra for greasing
2 eggs
400g (14oz) plain flour, plus extra for dusting
1/4 teaspoon fine salt
2 tablespoons soured cream or crème fraîche
100g (3½oz) caster sugar
2 teaspoons baking powder
1/4 teaspoon vanilla bean paste or extract
icing sugar, for dusting
Chantilly Cream (see page 165) or vanilla ice cream, to serve (optional)

FOR THE APPLES
1.3kg (3lb) tart apples - a mix of Braeburn, Granny Smith and Golden Delicious
2 teaspoons sugar
1/4 teaspoon vanilla bean paste or extract
2 teaspoons ground cinnamon, plus extra (optional) for sprinkling

Put all the main ingredients into the bowl of a stand mixer fitted with a paddle attachment. Mix on low speed until sandy, then turn out onto a work surface and knead until it comes together into a dough.

Divide the dough into 2 pieces, one just slightly larger than the other, and shape each into a log. Wrap each piece in nonstick baking paper and place in the freezer for at least 1 hour. (The recipe can be prepared up to this point one day in advance.)

When you're ready to cook the pie, remove the dough from the freezer, then preheat the oven to 180°C, 160°C fan (350°F), Gas Mark 4. Grease a 23cm (9 inch) round springform tin and dust with flour.

Peel, quarter and core the apples. Using a mandoline, carefully slice the apple pieces thinly into a bowl. Add the sugar, vanilla and cinnamon and toss together gently. Set aside.

Cut the larger dough piece into slices about 5mm (1/4 inch) thick, arrange them over the base of the tin and press down to seal the seams and create an even base layer of dough. Arrange the apple slices over the dough base, distributing them evenly up to the edges.

Using the largest holes of a box grater, grate the smaller dough piece over the apples to cover completely. At this point your tin may be close to overflowing, but the apples and dough settle in cooking, so continue grating as high as possible.

Bake for 40 minutes, then check and cover the top with foil if it's browning too quickly before baking for another 20–25 minutes until golden brown.

Remove from the oven and leave to cool before releasing from the tin. Serve at room temperature, dusted with icing sugar, with Chantilly Cream sprinkled with cinnamon or vanilla ice cream, if desired.

CREPES WITH APPLE MOUSSE
NALEŚNIKI RAIMUNDY Z PRAŻONYM JABŁKIEM

Crepes are very common fare in many Polish households, with both sweet and savoury fillings, and this recipe comes from my dear friend Raimunda. The batter is a bit thinner than the French crepes most people are familiar with, and the sparkling water gives them extra lightness. This simple apple filling takes me straight back to my grandmother's kitchen. A lovely example of Polish home cooking at its best.

MAKES 10–12 CREPES

1kg (2lb 4oz) tart cooking apples, such as Bramley, peeled and chopped
1 vanilla pod, split
60g (2¼oz) caster sugar, or more to taste
icing sugar, for dusting
mint leaves, to decorate

FOR THE CREPES
250ml (9fl oz) whole milk
250g (9oz) plain flour
2 eggs
250ml (9fl oz) sparkling water, or use plain
pinch of salt
4 teaspoons vegetable oil, plus extra (if needed) for cooking
pinch of ground cinnamon

Put the apples into a heavy-based pan with a lid, add the vanilla pod and sugar and pour in water to cover barely halfway. Bring just to a simmer and stir, then cover with the lid and cook over a very low heat for 30–40 minutes until completely soft and golden, stirring frequently. You can mash the apples with a wooden spoon if desired. Taste and adjust for sweetness with extra sugar. Set aside.

For the crepes, put all the ingredients into a mixing bowl and mix together until smooth. Leave to rest for 10 minutes.

Heat a nonstick frying pan or crepe pan and oil lightly, if necessary. When hot, pour a ladleful of batter into the pan, swirling to spread evenly, and cook over a medium heat until golden. Turn and cook the other side until golden, then transfer to a plate. Keep the cooked crepes covered with a clean tea towel while you cook the rest of the batter.

Spoon some apple mousse onto each warm crepe, then fold the crepe over in half and then in half again. Serve with a liberal dusting of icing sugar and a few mint leaves to decorate.

CHOUX CAKE WITH PASTRY CREAM & RHUBARB KARPATKA

This classic Polish layered cake is named after the Carpathian Mountains, and one glance explains why as it is all craggy and uneven. The crème pâtissière (pastry cream) is next-level from the addition of extra butter, while the rhubarb adds a gorgeous tartness that cuts through the richness, reminding me of my grandmother's garden-fresh rhubarb stalks. It's an absolute showstopper that tastes even better than it looks.

SERVES 6

FOR THE PASTRY CREAM
500ml (18fl oz) whole milk
1 vanilla pod, split
5 egg yolks
100g (3½oz) caster sugar
60g (2¼oz) cornflour
175–190g (6–7oz) unsalted butter, softened

FOR THE RHUBARB
220g (7¾oz) rhubarb, preferably forced pink, cut into pieces
4 tablespoons sugar
finely grated zest and juice of ½ orange
100ml (3½fl oz) water
1 tablespoon cornflour

FOR THE CHOUX BASE
200g (7oz) plain four, plus extra for dusting if needed
1 teaspoon baking powder
pinch of salt
200ml (7fl oz) water
130g (4½oz) unsalted butter, plus extra for greasing
4 eggs
icing sugar, for dusting

For the pastry cream, heat the milk with the vanilla pod in a saucepan until scalding (just before boiling). Remove from the heat and leave to infuse for 15 minutes.

Meanwhile, whisk together the egg yolks, sugar and cornflour in a heatproof bowl until well blended.

Scrape the seeds from the vanilla pod into the warm milk (see Note, page 210), then reheat until scalding.

Pour half the hot vanilla milk into the egg mixture while whisking constantly, then pour the hot egg mixture into the pan of remaining hot milk, scraping well to ensure all of it transfers. Cook over a medium heat, stirring constantly, until the mixture thickens and bubbles, then continue cooking and whisking for another 30 seconds. Remove from the heat and transfer to a shallow dish or large, wide mixing bowl, then dot the surface with 25–40g (1–1½oz) of the butter. Cover the surface with damp nonstick baking paper to prevent a skin from forming, then leave to cool to room temperature.

Cut the remaining 150g (5½oz) butter into small cubes. Using a hand-held electric mixer, beat the butter into the pastry cream, bit by bit, until well blended. Cover the surface again with damp baking paper and refrigerate until you are ready to assemble the cake.

For the rhubarb, put all the ingredients except the cornflour into a saucepan, cover with a lid and simmer gently for 3–5 minutes until only just tender. Strain the cooking juices into a bowl and mix in the cornflour until well blended. Return to the pan and set aside until ready to serve.

Continued overleaf

For the choux base, preheat the oven to 180°C, 160°C fan (350°F), Gas Mark 4. Select 2 x 20cm (8 inch) round springform cake tins.

Mix together the flour, baking powder and salt in a small bowl. Heat the measured water and butter in a saucepan over a low heat, stirring until the butter has melted. Add the flour mixture and cook, beating vigorously with a wooden spoon, until the mixture forms a sticky ball. Continue cooking and stirring for a minute or so until the mixture comes away from the sides of the pan. Remove from the heat and add the eggs, one at a time, beating thoroughly after each addition. The dough will be sticky, but smooth and glossy (you could also do this using a stand mixer).

Divide the mixture between the cake tins and smooth up to the edges but leave the surface bumpy, to resemble mountains. Bake for 30–40 minutes until puffed and golden. Remove from the oven and leave the cakes to cool completely in the tins before releasing.

To assemble, spread one of the cake layers with the pastry cream, then top with the other layer. Sift over a generous layer of icing sugar and accompany with the rhubarb.

CHANTILLY CREAM ROULADE
ROLADA Z BITĄ ŚMIETANĄ

This cake was compulsory at family gatherings when I was a child. My parents, my uncles, my aunties – everyone made it for fancy meals. There would be steak tartare to start (always), and then this would arrive and a hush would fall over us kids. I especially loved that glistening jewel of strawberry jelly running through the cream when it was sliced. At least that's how it felt to me. I still get a little thrill when I slice into one now. It's easy to make, and people of all ages are always impressed when I serve this.

SERVES 6–8

1 packet of strawberry or raspberry jelly
150g (5½oz) plain flour
½ teaspoon baking powder
5 eggs, separated
100g (3½oz) caster sugar, plus extra for sprinkling
icing sugar, for dusting
mint leaves, to decorate (optional)
sliced strawberries, to serve

FOR THE CHANTILLY CREAM
375ml (13fl oz) cold double cream
seeds scraped from 1 split vanilla pod (see Note, page 210)
2 tablespoons caster or icing sugar

The day before baking, prepare the jelly according to the packet instructions. Line a loaf tin (or similar rectangular dish) with clingfilm, leaving some excess overhanging the sides. Pour the jelly into the lined tin and chill for 6–8 hours or overnight until completely set.

The day of serving, preheat the oven to 200°C, 180°C fan (400°F), Gas Mark 6. Line a 30 x 40cm (12 x 16 inch) baking tray with nonstick baking paper.

Sift the flour and baking powder together. Set aside.

Put the egg whites into the bowl of a stand mixer fitted with a whisk attachment and beat until they begin to form stiff peaks. Reduce the speed and add the egg yolks, one at a time, beating well after each addition, then beat in the caster sugar.

Remove the bowl from the mixer and gently fold in the flour mixture using a spatula or large metal spoon.

Spread the batter evenly onto the lined tray and bake for 10–15 minutes until lightly golden and springy to the touch. Remove from the oven.

Lay a clean sheet of nonstick baking paper on the work surface and sprinkle lightly with sugar to help prevent sticking. Invert the cake onto the paper and peel off the lining paper. While the cake is still hot and starting from one long side, roll up the sponge tightly, rolling the cake and sugared paper together to form a log. Leave to cool completely.

Continued overleaf

When ready to assemble, lift the jelly from the tin using the excess clingfilm and cut it into a long, thin strip about 40cm (16 inches) long and 2cm (¾ inch) wide to fit the length of the cake – you will need to cut 2 strips; it's not a problem if there is a join inside the cake. Save any leftover jelly to enjoy another time!

Put the cream, vanilla seeds and sugar into the cleaned bowl of the stand mixer and beat until the mixture holds firm peaks.

Unroll the sponge and spread the Chantilly cream evenly over it. Lay the jelly strips in a line about 5cm (2 inches) in from the long side nearest to you. Using the paper beneath the sponge to help, begin from the end with the jelly and carefully roll up tightly to enclose the jelly. Trim the ends of the roll at an angle to reveal the jelly strip and to neaten.

Transfer to a serving plate, seam-side down. Chill until needed, then dust generously with icing sugar just before serving. Slice and serve with extra Chantilly cream on the side, decorated with mint leaves, if desired, and strawberry slices.

PISTACHIO BABKA

My grandmother had a pistachio obsession, fuelled by a cousin in Switzerland who sent her pistachios in every form imaginable, well before they became trendy. I think of her whenever I see them, and this recipe is no exception. Two is the magic number here. The recipe takes two days to make (the dough is left overnight to rise in the fridge), so it's well worth preparing two loaves at once – one to enjoy and one to freeze.

MAKES 2 X 900G (2LB) LOAVES

200ml (7fl oz) whole milk
7g (1/4oz) sachet fast-action dried yeast
70g (2 1/2oz) caster sugar
2 eggs, at room temperature
110g (4oz) unsalted butter, melted and cooled, plus extra for greasing
1 teaspoon vanilla extract
500g (1lb 2oz) plain flour, plus extra for dusting
240g (8 1/2oz) pistachio cream
100g (3 1/2oz) shelled pistachio nuts, crushed
6 tablespoons orange marmalade
6 tablespoons boiling water

Gently warm the milk in a small saucepan until just tepid or in a microwavable bowl in a microwave. Add the yeast and 1 teaspoon of the sugar, whisk together with a fork and leave to stand for 5–10 minutes, or until you see little bubbles on the surface.

Put the eggs, remaining sugar, melted butter, vanilla and flour in the bowl of a stand mixer fitted with a dough hook. Mix on low speed just until evenly combined, then add the yeast mixture and mix for about 10 minutes until you have a smooth dough.

Remove the bowl from the mixer and cover with clingfilm. Leave the dough to rise in a warm place for 1–2 hours until it has almost doubled in size.

Transfer the dough to a clean work surface. Lightly grease your hands with butter and knead for about 5 minutes to strengthen the gluten. Return the dough to the bowl, cover with the clingfilm and refrigerate overnight.

The next day, generously grease 2 x 900g (2lb) loaf tins.

Cut the dough in half. Cover one half with the clingfilm and return to the fridge. Roll the dough piece out on a lightly floured work surface into a rectangle about 23 x 43cm (9 x 17 inches); this is an approximate guide. Spread over the pistachio cream in an even layer, followed by about 2 tablespoons of the pistachios.

Starting from the long side, roll up the dough tightly into a log to enclose the filling. Using a sharp knife, cut the roll lengthways in half so that you have 2 strands and the filling is exposed. Twist the strands together by folding one over the other. It's easier and prettier to keep the filling facing upwards when assembling the babka. Twist well, but know it will be messy, which is fine because it's the twists that make the lovely pattern. Fold the twisted dough in half to fit it in the greased tin, and tuck it in gently.

Continued overleaf

Cover loosely with a clean damp tea towel while you prepare the remaining dough piece in the same way. Leave the loaves to prove in a warm place for about 30 minutes.

Preheat the oven to 200°C, 180°C fan (400°F), Gas Mark 6.

Bake the loaves for about 30 minutes until nicely browned on top but not too dark.

Meanwhile, prepare the glaze by diluting the marmalade with the measured boiling water.

Remove the cooked babkas from the oven and transfer to a wire rack still in the tins. Brush the tops with the glaze, then sprinkle over the remaining pistachios. Leave to cool completely before serving.

NOTE: You can replace the pistachio cream filling with chocolate spread, or use any nut butter and scatter with chopped pieces of the corresponding nut.

SWEET CHEESE TWISTS
DROŻDŻÓWKI Z SEREM

My favourite after-school snack, I remember the delight of coming home to a batch of warm *drożdżówki* with their pillowy dough cradling pockets of sweet farmer's cheese (Twaróg). If I got my timing right, my grandmother would have them cooling on wire racks, their golden tops still glistening with sugary icing. Nowadays, I keep these on hand for a late-morning pick-me-up and each warm bite still transports me straight back to Grandma in the kitchen.

MAKES 10

150ml (5fl oz) whole milk
7g (¼oz) sachet fast-action dried yeast
40g (1½oz) caster sugar
350g (12oz) plain flour, plus extra for dusting
¼ teaspoon salt
50g (1¾oz) unsalted butter, melted and cooled
½ teaspoon vanilla bean paste or extract
1 egg
1 egg white
pinch of salt

FOR THE CHEESE FILLING
250g (9oz) Polish Twaróg cheese or cottage cheese
1 egg yolk
finely grated zest of 1 lemon
2 tablespoons sugar

FOR THE GLACÉ ICING
100g (3½oz) icing sugar
25ml (1fl oz) milk

Gently warm the milk in a small saucepan until just tepid or in a microwavable bowl in a microwave. Add the yeast and 1 teaspoon of the sugar, whisk together with a fork and leave to stand for 5–10 minutes, or until you see little bubbles on the surface.

Put the flour, salt, melted butter, remaining sugar, vanilla, yeast mixture and whole egg in the bowl of a stand mixer fitted with a dough hook and mix on low speed, scraping down the sides of the bowl regularly, for 3–5 minutes until the dough just comes away from the sides of the bowl.

Remove the bowl from the mixer and cover with a clean tea towel. Leave the dough to rise in a warm place for 1–2 hours until it has almost doubled in size.

Preheat the oven to 200°C, 180°C fan (400°F), Gas Mark 6. Line a large baking tray with nonstick baking paper. Mix the egg white with the salt.

For the filling, mix all the ingredients together in a bowl until creamy.

Turn the dough out onto a lightly floured work surface, knead briefly until smooth and then roll into a rectangle about 31 x 51 (12½ x 20 inches); this is an approximate guide.

Spread the filling over the dough almost to the edges, and enclose it by folding one long side to the middle, then folding the other long side on top of it, like a long, thin book. Roll, pressing lightly, to seal.

Continued overleaf

With a sharp knife, trim the short sides just to neaten. Measure the length of the filled dough and at the midpoint cut widthways into 2. Divide each half into 5 equal pieces, cutting widthways. Lifting one piece at a time, twist to create a bow shape and transfer to the lined tray, evenly spaced apart. Brush lightly with the egg white mixture.

Bake for 15–20 minutes until golden brown. Remove from the oven and transfer to a wire rack to cool.

For the glacé icing, mix the icing sugar and milk together in a bowl, then brush generously over the twists. Leave to set before serving.

CHOCOLATE GINGERBREAD CAKE
PIERNIK CZEKOLADOWY

I always thought gingerbread was too intimidating to attempt at home, then on one visit to my grandmother I watched her casually making one in her kitchen like it was nothing at all. The moment I returned to London I baked my first gingerbread, and wondered what all my fuss was about! It's so straightforward yet looks so dramatic. And the flavours: dark chocolate and prunes and spices (but no ginger in Polish gingerbread!). The perfect celebration cake.

SERVES 8

130g (4½oz) unsalted butter, plus extra for greasing
200g (7oz) dark brown soft sugar
2 teaspoons bicarbonate of soda
250ml (9fl oz) whole milk
3 eggs, beaten
300g (10½oz) plain flour, plus extra for dusting
2 teaspoons cocoa powder
1 teaspoon ground cloves
1 teaspoon ground cinnamon
1 teaspoon dried lavender
1 teaspoon vanilla extract
1 quantity Chocolate Prune Butter (see page 210) or Blackcurrant Cointreau Compote (see page 209)
nasturtium flowers and leaves, to decorate (optional)

FOR THE GANACHE
100g (3½oz) dark chocolate, 75% cocoa solids, finely chopped
300ml (10fl oz) double cream

Preheat the oven to 200°C, 180°C fan (400°F), Gas Mark 6. Grease a 20cm (8 inch) round springform cake tin and dust with flour.

Melt the butter in a saucepan over a low heat, then whisk in the sugar until blended. Remove from the heat, stir in the bicarbonate of soda and milk and continue stirring. Add the eggs, one at a time, stirring well after each addition. Then add the flour, cocoa, spices, lavender and vanilla and stir until just mixed.

Transfer to the prepared tin and smooth the top. Bake for 30–45 minutes until puffed and a skewer inserted into the centre comes out clean. Remove from the oven and leave to cool completely in the tin on a wire rack.

For the ganache, put the chocolate into a heatproof bowl. Heat the cream in a saucepan until scalding (just before boiling), then pour over the chocolate, stirring constantly until fully blended.

Slice the cake horizontally into 2 equal layers, then sandwich together with the Chocolate Prune Butter, or Blackcurrant Cointreau Compote, spreading any excess onto the sides and top. Set the cake on a wire rack over a tray and pour over the warm ganache for a glossy, smooth finish. Alternatively, cool the ganache completely by setting it on a tray or bowl full of ice cubes, stirring constantly until thick and cold. Use a long, thin spatula to spread the ganache decoratively over the top and sides of the cake. Leave to set fully before serving, decorated with nasturtium flowers and leaves, if desired.

BANANA BREAD WITH SPELT & CHOCOLATE

This isn't your typical banana bread. Instead of just hiding the fruit inside, this recipe celebrates it by placing a halved banana on top, where it caramelizes into a gorgeous toffee-like crown. It's the kind of detail that has people asking for the recipe before taking their first bite. Inside, a mix of flours, dark chocolate and dark muscovado sugar creates subtle depth and a grown-up edge. Despite these special touches, it couldn't be easier to make. A perfect treat for elevenses or afternoon tea.

SERVES 6–8

120g (4¼oz) unsalted butter, plus extra for greasing
110g (4oz) dark muscovado sugar
½ teaspoon vanilla bean paste or extract
1 teaspoon bicarbonate of soda
100ml (3½fl oz) whole milk
2 eggs, beaten
140g (5oz) spelt flour
140g (5oz) plain flour
2 overripe bananas, mashed, plus 1, halved lengthways, for the top
50g (1¾oz) dark chocolate, 75% cocoa solids, chopped, plus extra, grated, for decorating
Chantilly Cream (see page 165) or Greek yogurt, to serve

Preheat the oven to 200°C, 180°C fan (400°F), Gas Mark 6. Grease and line a 900g (2lb) loaf tin.

Melt the butter in a saucepan over a low heat, then remove from the heat and whisk in the sugar and vanilla until well blended. Stir in the bicarbonate of soda, followed by the milk and eggs, and whisk until the mixture is smooth.

Sift the flours together into a separate bowl. Using a spatula, gently fold into the cake mixture until just combined. Add the mashed bananas, then fold in the chocolate, stopping before the chocolate melts too much.

Transfer the batter to the prepared tin and arrange the banana halves, cut-side up, on top. Bake for 30 minutes. Check, and if the top is browning too quickly, cover securely with foil. Bake for another 15–20 minutes until a skewer inserted into the centre comes out clean.

Remove from the oven and leave to cool in the tin for 10 minutes, then turn out onto a wire rack to cool completely. Slice and serve topped with Chantilly Cream or Greek yogurt, with extra chocolate grated over.

PLUM CRUMBLE CAKE
DROŻDŻOWE ZE ŚLIWKAMI

This was the last cake I baked for my grandmother, that final summer when she asked me to make one for her. The request filled me with panic as our roles began to shift, but I also understood that she wanted to honour the kitchen bond we had always shared. I baked it in her preferred tin, with shaking hands, terrified she wouldn't like it, but to my surprise and relief she loved it. We cried together with joy and sang old songs, a moment I'll treasure forever.

SERVES 10–12

250ml (9fl oz) whole milk
7g (1/4oz) sachet fast-action dried yeast
85g (3oz) caster sugar
500g (1lb 2oz) plain flour, plus extra for dusting
1/4 teaspoon salt
50g (1 3/4oz) unsalted butter, melted and cooled, plus extra for greasing
1 teaspoon vanilla extract
1 egg
3 egg yolks
800g (1lb 12oz) plums, halved and stoned

FOR THE CRUMBLE
100g (3 1/2oz) plain flour
80g (3oz) caster sugar
80g (3oz) cold unsalted butter, cut into small cubes

TO SERVE
roasted plums (see Note)
Greek yogurt

NOTE: Prepare your roasted plums as for the apricots on page 26.

Gently warm the milk in a small saucepan until just tepid or in a microwavable bowl in a microwave. Add the yeast and 1 teaspoon of the sugar, whisk together with a fork and leave to stand for 5–10 minutes, or until you see little bubbles on the surface.

Put the flour, salt, melted butter, remaining sugar, vanilla and whole egg in the bowl of a stand mixer fitted with a dough hook. Mix on low speed just until evenly blended. Add the yolks, one at a time, mixing well after each addition, then mix in the yeast mixture, scrape down the sides of the bowl and mix for about 10 minutes until you have a smooth dough.

Remove the bowl from the mixer and cover with a clean tea towel. Leave the dough to rise in a warm place for 1–2 hours until it has almost doubled in size.

Meanwhile, for the crumble, mix the flour and sugar together in a mixing bowl. Add the butter and rub in with your fingertips until the mixture resembles breadcrumbs.

Preheat the oven to 200°C, 180°C fan (400°F), Gas Mark 6. Grease a 23cm (9 inch) round springform cake tin and dust it with flour. Line a large baking tray with nonstick baking paper.

Transfer the dough to the cake tin and spread it out to fill. Arrange the plums on top, cut-side up, then sprinkle the crumble mix over the top. Stand the tin on the lined tray to catch any plum juice drips and bake for 40 minutes. Check, and if the top is browning too quickly, cover with foil. Bake for another 20–30 minutes until a skewer inserted in the centre comes out clean.

Remove from the oven and leave to cool completely in the tin on a wire rack. Serve with roasted plums and Greek yogurt.

FRENCH TOAST

Sweet yeast breads are a common feature of the Polish kitchen and so are ways to use any leftovers or stale slices. It is common to mix cinnamon with the egg batter, but I prefer to keep it fruity with orange. This makes it easy to serve with your favourite fresh fruit as a topping, though the roasted apricots on page 26 work well here, as does a spoonful or two of the Blackcurrant Cointreau Compote on page 209.

SERVES 2

2 eggs
50ml (2fl oz) whole milk
50ml (2fl oz) double cream
finely grated zest and juice of ½ orange, including pulp
¼ teaspoon vanilla bean paste
1 tablespoon sugar
4 thick slices of stale brioche
20–30g (¾–1oz) unsalted butter or clarified butter
icing sugar, for dusting
fresh fruit, to serve

Whisk together the eggs, milk, cream, orange zest and juice, vanilla and sugar in a large shallow dish or pan.

Add 2 slices of brioche to the egg mixture and leave to soak for about 1 minute each side.

Melt half the butter in a nonstick frying pan, add the 2 soaked bread slices and cook over a medium heat for about 2–3 minutes on each side until golden. Remove from the pan. Repeat for the remaining bread slices.

Serve immediately, dusted with icing sugar and accompanied by your favourite fresh fruit.

SWEET BLUEBERRY PIEROGI
PIEROGI Z JAGODAMI

Summer at the height of berry season in Poland meant one thing: fresh, sweet pierogi filled with bilberries, a sort of European wild blueberry. I remember watching my grandmother roll the dough paper-thin and cut perfect circles. Her hands moved with practised grace, placing berries in the centre of each and pinching the edges into flawless crescents. She would boil them until they rose to the surface, then toss them in butter and more berries. Polish summer in every bite, available year-round now, thanks to Grandma's recipe and frozen berries.

MAKES 30–40 PIEROGI

250g (9oz) plain flour, plus extra for dusting
125ml (4fl oz) hot water
2 tablespoons vegetable oil
pinch of salt

FOR THE FILLING
400g (14oz) fresh or frozen blueberries or bilberries
2 tabespoons sugar

TO SERVE
40g (1½oz) butter, melted
soured cream
mint leaves and sprigs, to decorate

Sift the flour into a mixing bowl. Add the measured hot water, oil and salt. Mix with a wooden spatula until the dough is cool enough to handle.

Transfer to a lightly floured work surface. Knead the dough vigorously for 10 minutes. Cover with a damp tea towel and leave to rest for 15 minutes.

Meanwhile, for the filling, mix the berries and sugar together well in a bowl.

Divide the dough into quarters. Working with one quarter at a time, and keeping the unrolled pieces covered by the damp tea towel, roll out the dough evenly so that you can just about see your hands through it. Using an upturned glass with a rim 7–9cm (2¾–3½ inches) in diameter, cut out as many circles as you can from the dough. You can reroll the scraps to cut out more.

Place a small spoonful of filling on each circle and fold the dough over in half to enclose the filling. Don't overfill or they may burst when cooking. Press the edges together to seal well. For a decorative edge, work around it pinching and then folding bit by bit. Alternatively, press around the edge with the tines of a fork to create a pattern, or just leave it plain.

As they are completed, place each filled and well-sealed pierogi on a lightly floured tray ready to cook. Line a separate tray with kitchen paper.

Bring a large saucepan of water to the boil, then reduce to a gentle simmer. Add the pierogi, in batches of 5 or 6, and cook for about 3–5 minutes until they bob up to the surface. Remove with a slotted spoon and leave to drain on the lined tray while you finish cooking all the pierogi.

To serve, transfer to a platter and top with any remaining berries, drizzle with the melted butter, decorate with mint leaves and sprigs and accompany with soured cream.

SWEET STRAWBERRY NOODLES
MAKARON Z TRUSKAWKAMI

This may seem an unlikely combo but, as every Polish child knows, noodles with fruit are the essence of summer in Poland. This works equally well with blueberries.

SERVES 2–4

- 500g (1lb 2oz) strawberries, hulled and halved
- 4 tablespoons sugar
- 6 tablespoons Greek yogurt or soured cream
- mint sprigs and leaves, to decorate

FOR THE NOODLES

- 125g (4½oz) plain flour, plus extra for dusting
- 1 egg plus 1 egg yolk, beaten together
- 25m (1fl oz) water
- 1 teaspoon vegetable oil

For the noodles, mound the flour on a clean work surface and make a well in the middle. Add the eggs, then gradually work in the flour. Add the measured water and the oil and continue mixing until you can form the rough dough into a ball. Dust lightly with flour, if sticky, and knead vigorously for 3–5 minutes until smooth. Shape into a ball, cover with an upturned bowl and leave to rest for 15–20 minutes.

Meanwhile, combine the strawberries and sugar in a mixing bowl and mash together gently. Stir in the yogurt or soured cream. Set aside.

Bring a saucepan of water to the boil.

Roll the dough out on a lightly floured work surface as thinly as you can without tearing. Roll the dough sheet up into a long tube and cut across into 5mm (¼ inch) pieces. Unravel the noodles, add to the boiling water and cook for about 3 minutes until they rise to the surface.

Drain the noodles and put onto a large plate. Leave to cool, then top with the strawberry mixture. Decorate with mint sprigs and leaves and serve.

PRUNE ICE CREAM

If I were a poet, I would write endless poems about prunes and their beauty and incredible flavour. But since I'm a cook, I use them in the kitchen instead. My grandmother knew about my prune obsession. In late summer, at the peak of the drying season, she would make me this ice cream using prunes still fresh and soft enough to meld gently with the cream. The flavour needs to be experienced; I'm genuinely envious of anyone tasting this for the first time.

SERVES 6–8

450ml (16fl oz) whipping cream
150ml (5fl oz) whole milk, plus a little (optional) extra
½ vanilla pod, split
5 egg yolks
50g (1¾oz) caster sugar
350g (12oz) soft pitted prunes, finely chopped
chopped pistachio nuts, to serve

NOTE: Alternatively, you can use an ice-cream maker to freeze/churn the custard, following the manufacturer's instructions, adding the prunes for the last few minutes of churning.

Put the cream, milk and vanilla pod into a saucepan and bring just to a simmer over a low heat. Remove from the heat.

Heat a little water in a small saucepan to a gentle simmer.

Select a heatproof mixing bowl that will, in due course, sit over the pan of simmering water without its base touching the water. Add the egg yolks and sugar to the bowl. Using a hand-held electric mixer, whisk together until pale and fluffy. Using a large serving spoon, gradually add the very hot cream mixture to the yolk mixture, one spoonful at a time, mixing vigorously after each addition to prevent curdling.

Set the bowl over the simmering water, making sure the base doesn't touch the water, and stir the mixture constantly with a wooden spoon until it is thick enough to coat the back of the spoon. To test for doneness, run your finger along the back of the spoon and the custard should hold the mark.

Pour the mixture through a sieve into a shallow freezerproof container with a lid. Leave to cool, then cover with the lid and place in the freezer. Remove every 30 minutes and stir with a fork to break up the crystals. After about 1½ hours, stir in the prunes. Continue stirring at regular intervals for another 1½ hours (3 hours total), or until the ice cream is fully set. Alternatively, freeze in the lidded container without stirring. When ready to serve, remove from the freezer and leave to soften slightly. Chop into small cubes and put into a food processor. Add a splash of milk and pulse until smooth. You may need to work in batches.

To serve, remove from the freezer and leave until soft enough to scoop. Scoop into bowls and sprinkle with chopped pistachios.

MY GRANNY'S FRUIT & PISTACHIO BISCOTTI

My grandmother was inspired to make biscotti after a visit to the Vatican, but unable to find a recipe on her return to Poland, she crafted her own using prunes, pistachios and spelt flour, plus a cheeky splash of vermouth. I've added generous amounts of dried figs and apricots for a wonderfully fruity bite. Unlike rock-hard traditional biscotti, these are intentionally much gentler on the teeth and perfect for dunking in coffee or tea or, as my grandmother did, in a glass of vermouth.

MAKES 20–30 BISCOTTI

150g (5½oz) soft pitted prunes
150g (5½oz) soft dried apricots
150g (5½oz) soft dried figs
50g (1¾oz) pistachio nuts
150g (5½oz) plain flour
100g (3½oz) spelt flour, plus extra for dusting
1 level teaspoon baking powder
¼ teaspoon fine salt
2 eggs, plus 1, beaten, for glazing
1 teaspoon vanilla extract
100g (3½oz) light brown soft sugar
40g (1½oz) butter, melted and cooled
25ml (1fl oz) red vermouth (or amaretto or sweet white wine)

Preheat the oven to 200°C, 180°C (400°F), Gas Mark 6. Line a baking tray with nonstick baking paper.

Halve all the dried fruits lengthways and mix with the pistachios in a bowl. Set aside.

Sift the flours, baking powder and salt into a large mixing bowl.

In a separate mixing bowl, beat together the eggs, vanilla, sugar, melted butter and vermouth until well mixed and smooth.

Pour the egg mixture into the flour mixture and, using a spatula, stir to form a rough dough. Stir in the dried fruit mixture.

Turn the dough out onto a generously floured work surface and knead briefly. Shape into a log approximately 2cm (¾ inch) high. Place the dough log on the lined tray, brush generously with the beaten egg and bake for 30 minutes. Check, and if the dough is not quite browned, continue baking for another 10 minutes.

Remove from the oven and leave to cool until just warm enough to handle. Reduce the oven temperature to 180°C, 160°C fan (350°F), Gas Mark 4.

Using a sharp knife, slice diagonally into pieces 1.5–2cm (⅝–¾ inch) thick. Arrange the slices on the baking tray and return to the oven for 10 minutes.

Remove from the oven, transfer to a wire rack and leave to cool completely before serving. Store wrapped in nonstick baking paper.

JAM COOKIES
CIASTECZKA Z DŻEMEM

When my grandmother made these, she would have used her homemade rose petal jam as the filling, but any flavour of preserve will work. The Blackcurrant Cointreau Compote on page 209 also makes an excellent filling. These are perfect with a cup of tea in the afternoon.

MAKES ABOUT
36 COOKIES

220g (7¾oz) unsalted butter, softened
120g (4¼oz) icing sugar, plus extra for dusting
¼ teaspoon vanilla bean paste or extract
4 egg yolks
pinch of fine salt
300g (10½oz) plain flour
30g (1oz) cornflour
raspberry, strawberry or apricot jam, or some of each, for the filling

Preheat the oven to 200°C, 180°C fan (400°F), Gas Mark 6. Line a large baking tray with nonstick baking paper.

Put the butter, sugar, and vanilla into the bowl of a stand mixer fitted with a paddle attachment and mix on high speed until the mixture is light and lemon-coloured. Add the egg yolks, one at a time, with the salt, beating well after each addition.

Add the flour and cornflour and mix until the dough comes together. If the dough is very soft, refrigerate for 20–30 minutes before rolling.

Divide the dough in half and refrigerate one half. Roll the other half into a log about 5cm (2 inches) in diameter. Cut small pieces, roughly 2–3cm (¾–1¼ inches) wide, from the log and shape into walnut-sized balls, about 20g (¾oz) each. Arrange, evenly spaced, on the lined tray. Use your thumb to make an indent in the middle of each round and then, using a teaspoon, fill with the jam of your choice. Do not overfill.

Bake for 10–15 minutes until the cookies just begin to brown around the edges. Remove from the oven, transfer to a wire rack and leave to cool completely. Repeat with the remaining dough.

When cool, dust the cookies with icing sugar.

CHAPTER 6

COCKTAILS

FRESH TOMATO BLOODY MARY

This was my grandfather Emil's summer drink, created during after-work gatherings in the back garden. With a greenhouse full of ripe tomatoes nearby, he would concoct these elixirs for himself and his mates, sneaking in vodka and lemon away from my grandmother's watchful eye. For the best results, use ripe summer tomatoes. In winter, when tomatoes are bland, add a dash of Worcestershire and Tabasco to bring everything to life.

MAKES 1

1 ripe tomato, chilled
50ml (2fl oz) vodka, preferably lemon vodka, chilled
1 tablespoon freshly squeezed lemon juice, or more to taste
salt and freshly ground black pepper

TO GARNISH
1 small red chilli, pimiento-stuffed olives

Using the largest holes of a box grater, grate the tomato into a small mixing bowl. Stir in the vodka, lemon juice and salt and pepper and mix together well. Taste and adjust the seasoning, adding extra salt and pepper and lemon juice as desired.

Pour into a glass, garnish with the chilli and olives and serve.

APPLE PIE

A classic Polish cocktail. I remember watching my parents and grandparents sipping this when I was young and it seemed the height of sophistication. The origins of the name are unclear, but the point is that the apple juice obscures the alcohol and makes this go down easily. Use good-quality juice for a nicer drink and you really should use Polish Zubrowka vodka for authentic flavour.

MAKES 1

100ml (3½fl oz) best-quality apple juice
50ml (2fl oz) Zubrowka vodka
1 teaspoon freshly squeezed lemon juice
ice cubes

TO GARNISH
lemon slice, basil sprig

Put the apple juice, vodka and lemon juice into a glass and stir to mix. Add ice cubes to top up.

Garnish with a lemon slice and basil sprig and serve.

WOJTEK'S COSMO

This was an acquired taste for me at the outset, but once I got the bug, I made sure to sample Cosmopolitans in every bar my travels took me to, from Warsaw to New York, from Saigon to London. For me, the secret is lime vodka and freshly squeezed lime juice, and keep it fruity with Cointreau rather than triple sec.

MAKES 1

ice cubes
juice of 2 limes
25ml (1fl oz) lime vodka
50ml (2fl oz) Cointreau
50ml (2fl oz) good-quality cranberry juice
orange zest, to garnish

Fill a cocktail shaker with ice and add all the ingredients except the garnish. Shake well and strain into a glass.

Garnish with orange zest and serve.

VERMOUTH TUTTI FRUTTI

My grandmother's favourite 'emergency' drink, I call it Tutti Frutti as she loved her vermouth infused with fruit in the summer. The cucumber is a nod to a Pimm's cup. Outside of the summer months you can use frozen berries for sunny joy all year round (see photograph opposite).

MAKES 1

ice cubes
handful of mixed berries
50ml (2fl oz) sweet vermouth
150ml (5fl oz) good-quality tonic water, plus extra to serve
1 baby cucumber slice
1 orange zest strip

Fill a glass halfway with ice cubes, add the berries and vermouth and fill up with tonic water.

Add the cucumber and orange zest to the glass and serve with extra tonic to top up.

ELDERFLOWER ROSE SPRITZ

A light and refreshing drink for hot days. There is something so appealing about the colour and taste of rose syrup, but if you prefer, replace it with hibiscus or pomegranate syrup. Also, any fizz will work here: you could opt for a Spanish cava, a French crémant or dry white wine, or keep it all pink with a rosé.

MAKES 1 LARGE OR 2 SMALL

50ml (2fl oz) elderflower cordial
100ml (3½fl oz) prosecco
100ml (3½fl oz) good-quality tonic water
2 teaspoons rose syrup
ice cubes

Mix all the ingredients together, adding the syrup last due to its thickness.

Pour into a large glass or 2 small glasses filled with ice cubes and serve.

FRUIT LIQUEURS
LIKIERY OWOCOWE

These are typically Polish and here are some of my favourite flavours. Serve neat or over ice with tonic water as a spritz. Liqueurs were my grandmother's speciality, reserved exclusively for visits from her girlfriends. She served them in beautiful cut-glass decanters that set off their rich, intense colours, prompting my grandfather to call them, jokingly, her 'perfumes'. Store in a cool, dry place.

REDCURRANT LIQUEUR

MAKES ABOUT 750ML (1¹/₃ PINTS)

500g (1lb 2oz) redcurrants, destemmed
500ml (18fl oz) vodka
300g (10½oz) caster sugar

Put the redcurrants into a tall 2 litre (3½ pint) sterilized jar with a tight-fitting lid (see Note). Pour over the vodka and seal. Leave to infuse for 2 weeks in a warm place.

Strain the infused vodka through a muslin cloth into a large sterilized jar. Put the redcurrants into a separate sterilized jar along with the sugar and stir to mix. Seal and set aside for 3–5 days until a ruby syrup forms.

Strain the fruit syrup through a fine-mesh sieve into the infused vodka and reseal.

QUINCE LIQUEUR

MAKES ABOUT 1 LITRE (1¾ PINTS)

1kg (2lb 4oz) quinces, peeled, cored and quartered
500g (1lb 2oz) caster sugar
1 litre (1¾ pints) good-quality vodka

Layer the quinces and sugar in a large sterilized jar with a tight-fitting lid (see Note), trimming the fruit pieces further to fit if necessary. Pour over the vodka and seal. The sugar should dissolve within 24 hours, but if not, give the jar a gentle shake occasionally to help it along. Leave to infuse for about 4 weeks.

Strain through a muslin cloth into a sterilized bottle and seal.

SOUR CHERRY LIQUEUR

MAKES ABOUT 600ML (1 PINT)

300g (10½oz) dried sour cherries
150g (5½oz) caster sugar
600ml (1 pint) vodka

Put the cherries and sugar into a tall 1 litre (1¾ pint) sterilized jar with a tight-fitting lid (see Note). Seal and shake to coat the fruit with the sugar.

Pour over the vodka and stir gently until the sugar begins to dissolve. Reseal and leave for 4–6 weeks to infuse. Strain the vodka through a muslin cloth into a large sterilized bottle and seal.

NOTE: To sterilize jars and bottles and their lids, preheat the oven to 140°C, 120°C (275°F), Gas Mark 1. Wash thoroughly in hot, soapy water, then rinse well and stand on a baking tray. Place in the oven for about 15 minutes. Since dry heat may damage any rubber seals, remove them and soak in boiling water for about 5 minutes to sterilize.

BARCELONA

CHAPTER 7

A POLISH PANTRY

HOMEMADE MAYONNAISE

I cannot deny that jars of shop-bought mayo are so handy, but nothing beats homemade mayonnaise, and it is a staple of the Polish kitchen. If you use a lot, double this recipe. If you like your mayo extra rich, add an extra yolk. The most important thing is to ensure all the ingredients are at the same temperature, which should be room temperature and not straight from the fridge.

MAKES ABOUT 250ML (9FL OZ)

1 egg, at room temperature
1 tablespoon cider vinegar or rice vinegar
1 teaspoon Dijon mustard, at room temperature
250ml (9fl oz) good-quality sunflower oil
fine salt

Select a tall, narrow jug or jar just large enough to hold a stick bender. Whisk the egg, vinegar and mustard together with a fork to blend, then add the oil.

Insert the stick blender into the jug or jar so that it is touching the bottom. Without tilting or moving the bender, turn it on high and blitz. As soon as the mixture begins to emulsify, lift out the blender but continue blitzing up to the top. Season to taste with salt.

Alternatively, put the egg, vinegar and mustard into a mixing bowl and whisk with a balloon whisk to blend. Begin pouring in the oil in a steady stream, whisking constantly, until emulsified and all the oil is incorporated. Season to taste with salt.

Cover and keep refrigerated until ready to use or serve.

POLISH PICKLED CUCUMBER

Of all the jars lining my grandmother's pantry shelves, these pickles disappeared the fastest, and I was usually the culprit. I simply could not resist that slight sweetness balanced with just the right amount of tang, made the Polish way, to absolute perfection. The hardest part is waiting the two weeks for the flavours to develop, but it's worth every day. Eat them straight from the jar, tuck them into a ham sandwich or serve them alongside mash and chicken schnitzel (see page 74) for a taste of Poland wherever you might be.

MAKES 3 X 250ML (9FL OZ) JARS

250ml (9fl oz) water
5 tablespoons distilled white vinegar
8 allspice berries
6 bay leaves
75g (2¼oz) caster sugar
3 teaspoons salt
2 large cucumbers
2 teaspoons Dijon mustard
½ teaspoon yellow mustard seeds

Sterilize 3 x 250ml (9fl oz) jars and their lids (see Note, page 200).

Put the measured water, vinegar, allspice berries, bay leaves, sugar and salt into a saucepan. Bring just to a simmer, stirring until the sugar has dissolved. Remove from the heat and leave to cool.

Cut the cucumbers into spears just long enough to fit upright in your sterilized jars up to below the rim. Arrange the cucumbers in the jars, packing them tightly. Add a bay leaf and an allspice berry from the brine to each jar.

Once the brine has cooled, stir in the mustard and mustard seeds until well combined. Pour the brine over the cucumbers, ensuring they are completely covered. Seal tightly and leave to cool, then keep refrigerated. Leave for 2 weeks before opening.

COURGETTE KETCHUP

My grandmother loved finding new ways to preserve courgettes, and knowing my tomato ketchup addiction, she set herself a challenge. Inspired by her neighbour Hanka, she created this courgette ketchup just for me. It's incredibly delicious as a condiment, but it's also so much more than that. Every time I make it, I'm reminded of how my grandma showed love through food, a gesture that moves me to this day.

MAKES ABOUT 3 X 280ML (9¾FL OZ) JARS

500g (1lb 2oz) courgettes, grated
1 small apple, cored and grated
250g (9oz) onion, finely chopped or grated
45g (1½oz) dark brown soft sugar
4 tablespoons cider vinegar
¼ teaspoon salt
1 teaspoon paprika
250g (9oz) tomato purée

Sterilize 3 x 280ml (9¾fl oz) jars and their lids (see Note, page 200).

Put the courgettes, apple and onion into a small heavy-based pan. Add the sugar, cover with a lid and simmer over the lowest heat for 20 minutes, stirring occasionally and ensuring the mixture does not catch on the bottom of the pan; stir in a splash of water if necessary.

Remove the lid, add the remaining ingredients and continue cooking, uncovered, for another 10 minutes. Taste and adjust for spiciness, saltiness, acidity and consistency.

Using a stick blender, blitz until smooth. Transfer to the sterilized jars, filling to the rim, and seal tightly. Leave to cool, then keep refrigerated.

TOMATO WOJTEK'S TOMATO JAM

Tomatoes were such a huge part of my childhood that I earned the nickname Tomato Wojtek, all thanks to my grandparents' greenhouse bursting with enough ripe beauties to feed the whole neighbourhood. Personal preference aside, there is something special about this unusual sweet jam and here's the best part: it's incredibly easy to make. In no time at all, you can bottle up summer.

MAKES ABOUT 3 X 280ML (9¾FL OZ) JARS

1kg (2lb 4oz) ripe tomatoes, chopped
250g (9oz) sugar
250g (9oz) preserving sugar
finely grated zest of 1 lemon
15g (½oz) fresh root ginger, peeled and grated
3 small red chillies (optional)

Sterilize 3 x 280ml (9¾fl oz) jars and their lids (see Note, page 200).

Put the tomatoes, sugars, lemon zest and ginger into a large saucepan and simmer gently, stirring frequently, for 45 minutes–1 hour until you obtain a jammy consistency.

Using a stick blender, blitz carefully until smooth. Then continue simmering for 10 minutes.

Put a chilli into each sterilized jar if desired. Spoon in the hot jam just to the rim and seal tightly. Leave to cool, then keep refrigerated.

BLACKCURRANT COINTREAU COMPOTE

My grandmother taught me to love the smell of blackcurrants simmering on the hob during hot summer days, and it's something I'll always treasure. When currant season hit its peak, she would make syrups and ice creams from black, white and red varieties, but this was always my favourite. She traditionally used vodka, though I've found the hint of orange from Cointreau enhances the berries beautifully. Serve this with French Toast (see page 181) or Crepes (see page 161), spread it on a buttered croissant, swirl it into porridge or spoon it over ice cream.

MAKES 2 X 225ML (8FL OZ) JARS

450g (1lb) fresh or frozen blackcurrants
75g ($2\frac{3}{4}$oz) caster sugar
2 bay leaves
50ml (2fl oz) Cointreau

Sterilize 2 x 225ml (8fl oz) jars and their lids (see Note, page 200).

Put all the ingredients into a heavy-based pan and bring just to a simmer, stirring to dissolve the sugar. Cover with the lid, then continue simmering for 30 minutes, stirring occasionally.

Ladle into the sterilized jars, adding a bay leaf to each, and seal tightly. Leave to cool, then keep refrigerated.

CHOCOLATE PRUNE BUTTER

This is what you will need for the Chocolate Gingerbread Cake on page 174, but you could also try it as a cheese board chutney alternative. When making this for a Christmas spread, I add cloves. Beware when cooking: the aroma of simmering prunes and cocoa will drive you wild.

MAKES ABOUT 500G (1LB 2OZ)

500g (1lb 2oz) soft prunes, pitted
200ml (7fl oz) vanilla vodka
200ml (7fl oz) water
1 split vanilla pod from the vanilla vodka or 1 vanilla pod, split
2 tablespoons cocoa powder
½ teaspoon ground cloves (optional)

Put the prunes, vodka, measured water and vanilla pod into a saucepan and bring just to the boil. Reduce the heat, cover the pan with a lid and simmer for 10 minutes.

Stir in the cocoa powder, and cloves if using, re-cover and simmer for another 5 minutes, or until thick, stirring occasionally.

Remove from the heat and fish out the vanilla pod (see Note). While still warm, blitz with a stick blender until completely smooth. Leave to cool, then transfer to a clean bowl, cover and keep refrigerated until you want to use it.

NOTE: Don't discard the vanilla pod: pat dry with kitchen paper and add to a jar of sugar to flavour it.

STAUB

PICKLED PEARS

I'll never forget the sight of pickled pears in my grandmother's cellar, those golden jars glowing among all the ruby red berries and preserves. Just know that patience is key here, as the flavours need about two weeks to develop fully. The pears may darken a bit as they sit, but that's perfectly normal and doesn't affect the amazing taste. Because the brine is made with cider vinegar, any leftovers mixed with soda water make a delicious drink, too.

MAKES 4 X 300ML (10FL OZ) JARS

250ml (9fl oz) cider vinegar
125g (4½oz) caster sugar
1 tablespoon cloves
2 cinnamon sticks, broken in half
600ml (1 pint) water
6 or 7 almost-ripe pears, peeled, cored and sliced

Sterilize 4 x 300ml (10fl oz) jars and their lids (see Note, page 200).

Put all the ingredients except the pears into a saucepan and bring just to a simmer.

Arrange the pear slices upright in the sterilized jars. Ladle in the hot brine, ensuring the pears are completely covered, then add some cloves and a piece of cinnamon from the brine to each. Seal tightly and leave to cool, then keep refrigerated.

PICKLED CHERRIES

What's not to love about these plump, jewel-like cherries steeped in a mild vinegar brine? They make a wonderful addition to a cheeseboard. The leftover brine is nice mixed with tonic as a spritz.

MAKES 2 X 380ML (13¾FL OZ) JARS

450g (1lb) cherries, stalks removed
6 tablespoons caster sugar
6 tablespoons rice vinegar

Sterilize 2 x 380ml (13¼fl oz) jars and their lids (see Note, page 200).

Fill the sterilized jars with cherries just to the rim. Divide the sugar and vinegar between the jars.

Bring a kettle of fresh water to the boil and pour into the jars with the cherries, ensuring they are completely covered. Seal tightly and leave to cool, then keep refrigerated.

PICKLED VEGETABLE TRIO

The three Polish pickled Rs – red cabbage, radish and red onion – are a great addition to almost every dish, from Pierogi (see page 104) to Egg Mayo (see page 30), so you should make these all the time and ensure a good stock is always in the fridge. This is a slightly sweet brine and I love it for everyday eating.

MAKES 3 X 380ML (13¾FL OZ) JARS

2 small red onions or 1 large, halved
¼ red cabbage
200g (7oz) radishes
3 bay leaves

FOR THE BRINE
2 teaspoons yellow mustard seeds
2 teaspoons black peppercorns
500ml (18fl oz) water
250ml (9fl oz) cider vinegar
200g (7oz) caster sugar

Sterilize 3 x 380ml (13¼fl oz) jars and their lids (see Note, page 200).

Using a mandoline or a sharp knife, slice each vegetable very thinly.

Put each of the sliced vegetables into their own sterilized jar and add a bay leaf to each. Keep covered while you prepare the brine.

Toast the mustard seeds and peppercorns in a dry saucepan over a low heat until you can smell the aroma. Add the remaining ingredients and bring just to a simmer over a low heat. Stir occasionally, and as soon as the sugar has dissolved, remove from the heat. Do not let the brine boil.

Pour the hot brine over the vegetables, dividing it between the jars, ensuring the contents are completely covered. Be sure to include an equal quantity of the mustard seeds and peppercorns in each; you may need to use a small spoon to distribute them evenly. Seal tightly and leave to cool, then keep refrigerated. These are ready to eat after 2 hours, but they will be better after 24 hours.

POLISH VEGETABLE BOUILLON
ROSÓŁ

This is the Queen of Broths, the Mother of Soups, where humble vegetables turn into liquid gold. It's deep in flavour, nourishing and essential. Add the chilli if you like to give it a bit of warmth.

MAKES ABOUT 1.5 LITRES (2¾ PINTS)

2 onions, halved
1 large parsnip, peeled and halved
2 large carrots, peeled and halved
½ small celeriac, peeled and roughly chopped
1 leek, trimmed, cleaned and halved
2–3 celery sticks, with leaves
2 tablespoons vegetable oil
2 litres (3½ pints) water
1 apple, halved
4 large garlic cloves, smashed
1 small bunch of flat leaf parsley
4 bay leaves
6 allspice berries
1 red chilli (optional)

Preheat the oven to 200°C, 180°C fan (400°F), Gas Mark 6. Line a large baking tray with nonstick baking paper.

Put the onions, parsnip, carrots, celeriac, leek and celery onto the lined tray, drizzle over the oil and toss to lightly coat. Spread out on the tray and roast for 20–30 minutes until coloured.

Transfer all the roasted vegetables to a large saucepan. Add all the remaining ingredients and bring to the boil, then reduce the heat and simmer for 30 minutes.

Leave to cool, then cover and refrigerate overnight.

The next day, strain and discard the vegetables. The bouillon is then ready to use, or freeze for future use.

STAUB

POLISH 'GNOCCHI' KOPYTKA

The Polish name translates to 'little hooves', and these soft, gooey dumplings are so much lighter than their Italian cousin, gnocchi, practically melting in your mouth with each bite. They're the perfect alternative to potatoes or grains, ready to soak up whatever delicious sauce you pair them with, whether that's a rich stew or a saucy meat dish (see page 90). Light yet filling, once you experience how pillowy and tender these are, you'll understand why they're such a beloved comfort food.

SERVES 2–4

750g (1lb 10oz) potatoes, such as Maris Piper, peeled and cut into evenly sized chunks
150g (5½oz) plain flour, plus extra for dusting
1 egg, beaten
vegetable oil
fine salt

Cook the potatoes in a saucepan of lightly salted boiling water for 15–20 minutes until tender. Drain and mash.

Bring a large saucepan of salted water to the boil, then reduce to a simmer and cover with a lid.

Put the warm mash, flour, egg and ¼ teaspoon salt into a mixing bowl. Using your hands, mix to a smooth dough. Turn out onto a clean work surface. If it is very sticky, you may need to dust your hands and the work surface with flour.

Divide the dough into quarters. Working with one quarter at a time, roll the dough into a long log about 3cm (1¼ inches) in diameter. Using a sharp knife, mark the log approximately every 2cm (¾ inch), then slice at an angle on the marks to create lots of diamond-shaped dumplings.

Add the dumplings to the boiling water and cook for 3–4 minutes until they all rise to the surface. Using a slotted spoon, transfer to a colander to drain, then toss very lightly with vegetable oil to prevent sticking. Repeat with the remaining dough quarters. Serve hot.

INDEX

GLOSSARY OF UK/US TERMS

bacon lardons – matchsticks of slab bacon
beetroot – beets
bicarbonate of soda – baking soda
butter beans – lima beans
caster sugar – superfine sugar
clingfilm – plastic wrap
cocktail stick – toothpick
cornflour – cornstarch
courgette – zucchini
double cream – heavy cream
flaked almonds – sliced almonds
frying pan – skillet
hob – stove
icing sugar – confectioners' sugar
minced – ground
peppers (green/red/yellow) – bell peppers
plain flour – all-purpose flour
prawn – shrimp
roasting tin – roasting pan
sieve – fine-mesh strainer
spring onions – green onions/scallions
stock – broth
sultanas – golden raisins
sweetcorn – corn
tea towel – dish towel
tomato purée – tomato paste

To my grandmother

AUTHOR'S ACKNOWLEDGEMENTS

Writing my very first cookbook, darting between recipe testing and a constant battle with imposter syndrome, it was the connection with my nearest and dearest that kept me going. Human connection is so valuable, whether it's the family we are born into or the one we choose; this book has made me realize that more than ever before. The support I have received throughout this process has been beyond measure.

This book is dedicated to my beloved grandmother Zofia who, against all the odds, never gave up and, as we say these days, 'powered through' her life but made it look effortless, proving that life is best lived that way. I feel so very lucky to be her eldest grandson. She shaped my way of looking at food – honestly – and my resourcefulness, and she never questioned my life choices.

There are three other incredible women that made this book so wonderful: Alison, my publishing director – you recognized the potential and took a chance on me. Working with you has been one of the greatest privileges and a dream come true. Yasia – your appreciation of beauty and Polish heritage helped to make this book look so spectacular. Laura, my wonderful, wise and ultra-diligent food editor – you made sure that it's impossible to cook any of these recipes any way but perfectly. Thank you for keeping up with me!

Heartfelt thanks also to: Ginger Pig and their wonderful local team at Lauriston Road – a sense of community is so important to me, and Nicola and her marketing team supported me throughout the process of writing this book, and shared so many kilos of meat, and also pearls of wisdom both brilliant and funny. Staub UK – their pots will be in my family for generations now, and to have their support for this special project was beyond precious, and symbolic, too. *Un grand merci!* Lia – who helped with the espresso yields for the brisket recipe. Raimunda – for sharing her crepes recipe and for always having an answer to my questions. Josh Spero, Lewis Hayward, Kristof Brument and Ashton Hugh – for capturing me in my element. And my darling George from Stevens of Sibsey – your flowers not only brighten my days, they also tell a wonderful story of trust, support and incredible kinship. I hope you are proud of how all your flowers have showed up on these pages!

Finally, thank you to the people who believed in me more than I believed in myself: Vezyris Vezyroglou – I have a tear in my eye as I recall all the moments of your support. *Efcharistó pará polí* for always showing up and being there for me, whether it was convenient or not. You are a fabulous, precious woman, and I am very lucky Instagram connected us. Peter Cha – a tireless believer in my capacity to make the world a tastier place. Your support means the world to me. Caroline – my fantastic coach who predicted this book's existence long before I could even think it might be possible! James H-K and Josh JFP – thank you for believing in me and supporting me to make this all happen. It wouldn't have been possible without you. My dear friends Karo and Agata – thank you for sticking up for me and being honest, in a Polish way, and unbiased. Life is easier with you. My TPV Gang, Becky and Barny – thank you for your exquisite taste and equally exquisite support. Your cheer has added so much to this book!

Lastly, to my wonderful mum, Mama Bozania. 'Just use common sense!' is always her answer when I ask for a recipe. I'm so glad there are people like you who cook by intuition, with the results always tasting exquisite – how precious you are.

Wojtek van Portek grew up in Poland in the 1980s, learning from his grandmother in the countryside about her traditional techniques of cooking and how to tend a vegetable garden – and why making a meal can be a simple yet generous act. In 2010, Wojtek moved to London to finish his studies in fashion and political science. Although he was working with some of fashion's biggest names, including Condé Nast as a fashion coordinator and Burberry as a stylist, he never stopped inventing recipes that combined his Polish heritage with London's global cuisines. Later, as Global Lead Stylist at fashion brand Reiss, he launched his Wojtek's Bistro supper club from his East London flat. It started as a homage to his upbringing, mixed with an elegant London sensibility, and acquired a cult following, attracting journalists, artists and fashion-industry executives through his @vanportek Instagram account. Wojtek is now Style Editor at *House & Garden.*

First published in Great Britain in 2026 by
Mitchell Beazley, an imprint of
Octopus Publishing Group Ltd
Carmelite House
50 Victoria Embankment
London EC4Y 0DZ
www.octopusbooks.co.uk

An Hachette UK Company
www.hachette.co.uk

The authorized representative in the EEA is
Hachette Ireland, 8 Castlecourt Centre,
Dublin 15, D15 XTP3, Ireland (email: info@hbgi.ie)

Photographs of the author: Page 5 Josh Spero, Page 10 Lewis Hayward, Page 11 Kristof Brument, Page 224 Ashton Hugh

Distributed in the US by Hachette Book Group
1290 Avenue of the Americas, 4th and 5th Floors
New York, NY 10104

Distributed in Canada by Canadian Manda Group
664 Annette St., Toronto, Ontario, Canada M6S 2C8

ISBN: 978-1-84601-678-3
eISBN: 978-1-84601-679-0

A CIP catalogue record for this book is available from the British Library.

Printed and bound in China.

MIX
Paper | Supporting responsible forestry
FSC www.fsc.org FSC® C008047

10 9 8 7 6 5 4 3 2 1

Photography & Styling: Wojtek van Portek

Publishing Director: Alison Starling
Contributing Editor: Laura Washburn
Project Editors: Sybella Stephens and Sarah Reece
Copy Editor: Jo Richardson
Art Director & Designer: Yasia Williams
Production Manager: Caroline Alberti